How to Fit in the Christian Society

And Why I No Longer Choose To

Dylan Glenn

Stark Stork Press

Copyright © 2024 Dylan Glenn

All rights reserved.

ISBN: 979-8-218-41679-9

Cover Art by Dylan Glenn

With thanks to Sami Glenn for her help in copy editing

Contents

Contents

"The result of dogmatic theology is a mockery of God."

-- Søren Kierkegaard

Introduction

"The weather is looking beautiful today."

"It sure is. God is good."

"God is good indeed. How can someone say God doesn't exist with weather like this?"

"Amen."

It is a bright Sunday morning at the neighborhood church, as Christians meander about after the sermon and engage in pleasant conversation. Someone in this particular interaction has just said something rather unreasonable. Out of politeness, apathy, or perhaps genuine agreement, his friend allowed the comment. In the name of Jesus Christ, two men who would never have ordinarily crossed paths find conversation over a batch of Sunday morning donuts.

Each Sunday, millions of Americans attend church, listen to sermons, and, most importantly, have pleasant conversations. Sometimes they talk about the kids, the family, or their annoying boss. Other times they discuss the sermon, share prayer requests, or make other religious remarks that go unchallenged. Some Christians at Sunday morning services legitimately believe in the resurrection of Jesus Christ 2,000 years ago, and some do not. Many are truly convinced that they will live a blissful afterlife, while others have never seriously reflected upon the idea. It could be that the two men I overheard actually think the weather provides proof of God's existence, or it could be that they simply wish to say something to their neighbor.

Rather evidently, Christianity functions not only as a personal way of life, but also as a social landscape. Within a Church community you will find benign conversations after Sunday sermons and friendly small talk before Wednesday night small groups. These interactions, unassuming as they may be, form the foundation of the characteristically warm Christian atmosphere that appeals to so many who crave community. Social belonging is not a just perk or appendage to Christianity, rather it is a core component of the religion that manifests week-in and week-out whenever Christians sing, pray, or converse with other Christians.

As someone who grew up in the Church, attending private Christian schools from preschool to 12th grade, I am very familiar with the born-again, hands in the air, Chris Tomlin-loving American Evangelical. I regularly attended Sunday services, weekly small groups, and yearly service trips. The Church was my life, and this life was as much about knowledge of the Bible as it was about playing youth group games with my friends.

Throughout my childhood, teachers and pastors would often tell me what it took to be a true Christian. They said that a true Christian did more than simply call themselves "Christian" or go to Church on Sundays. Rather, they lived their life striving towards righteousness, emulating the life of Christ, and believing in the gospel message. As I grew up observing the Church around me, the more I came to disagree with this well-meaning definition of a "true Christian."

Christians form a group, and, like any group, membership is defined by the acceptance of current members, not by adherence to a set of unchanging ideas. Throughout history, individuals have been regarded as true and legitimate Christians despite holding beliefs that were diverse, mutually incompatible, and even deeply un-Christlike. For instance, Christians who rallied courageously against the institution of slavery were just as Christian as those who condoned slavery's existence.[1] Christians who lived peacefully beside their Muslim neighbors were as genuinely Christian as those who burned heretics alive in extra-judicial inquisitions. Today, some groups of Christians claim that true admittance to the Faith requires

3

baptism; others say it only requires belief in the resurrection, and still others maintain that no belief in any dogma is required at all.[2] Even if you have conversed directly with God and hold the true, inspired, and exact criteria needed for someone to call themselves a "true believer," you must accept that less-inspired minds are met with many conflicting and equally certain definitions of Christianity.

As a purely descriptive observation, the bounds of the Church are defined by those already within it. My primary school teachers might have provided an excellent prescriptive definition for what a Christian *should* be, though I do not think they accurately described the reality of the situation. Functionally, being a Christian in society means nothing more than calling yourself "Christian" and going to Church on Sundays. These two acts alone are sufficient for membership into the group.

Community, in a very real sense, defines Christians. Christians follow God, and they find God in community with other believers. Christians also claim to find God in truth. In this book, I aim to convince you that a tension exists between these two paths to God: the path through community and the path through truth. I will argue that churches cultivate an incredibly fertile ground for the creation of deep relationships and strong social networks, and I will show that all Christians had to do to create such a wonderful society was sacrifice truth-seeking for tribalism.

GOD IN COMMUNITY

When I see others try to explain why they became a Christian, time and time again I have watched them struggle to provide a definitive answer. To explain a decision so consequential, people often want to provide a rationale that is objective, grounded, and reasonable. The allure of the Christian experience, however, is very often subjective, spiritual, and non-rational. If most Christians were to honestly analyze the roots of their faith, they would not find rigorous arguments or logical necessities pointing towards doctrinal truth. Instead, they would find memories of singing uplifting Christian songs, or recollections of connecting with friends at Wednesday night small group. After all, people do not become Christian because they believe Jesus rose from the dead; rather, they believe Jesus rose from the dead because they became Christian.

The fact that community contributes to many religious experiences and shapes many religious thoughts does not deny that many people hold profoundly singular convictions. A Christian hermit alone in the wilderness may well live as a true believer, but by being alone, the hermit misses out on the communal religious experiences that most Christians engage in and find God through. These spiritually fulfilling experiences include vulnerable conversations with friends, public service alongside colleagues, and emotionally captivating singing beside other believers. Without these communal rituals, the entire identity of Christianity would shift into something unrecognizable.[3]

If actions and policies that promote social cohesion lead to a fuller discovery of God, and discovery of God is a positive and desirable thing, then surely the Church should promote social cohesion to the maximum degree. There is at least one constraining factor: the truth.

GOD IN TRUTH

I could go on describing God as any number of things — God is creator, God is power, God is love, etc. — though I hope in equal plainness all can accept that the God of Christians corresponds with truth, or at least *should* correspond with truth. Jesus Christ, after all, did not merely bring truth and life; he said that he was himself the truth and the life.[4] The Bible depicts the adversary to the Lord (i.e. Satan) as the father of lies, and we are told to combat the force of lies with the belt of truth.[5] The closer we come to the truth, the closer we should come to the Christian God.

As it happens, modern society has discovered rather effective tools for discerning the truth. The whole of the Enlightenment legacy, which offered science as an antidote to superstition, rests on the value of questioning. Dogma or groupthink cannot serve as a reasonable basis for any kind of truth, and even if some truth did arise from these unlikely sources, we could not confirm the legitimacy of the truth claims until we had first made strong and persistent efforts to disprove them. As David Hume aptly put it, "truth springs from argument among friends." Very few people enjoy having their deeply held ideas challenged, but we must appreciate the value of those friends who push against our intellectual bubbles of certainty.

I see in the churches of this country a prevailing attitude of certainty. Instead of encouraging the kind of critical dialogue that leads to truth, Christian congregations instead tend to cultivate insular intellectual bubbles. There is nothing inherently harmful about finding comfort in certainty or spending time with agreeable friends, though we must recognize that these comforts are corrosive in excess. A Christian searching for God through skepticism and investigation will all too often butt heads with those who have already found God in their tight-knit community.

* * *

As you read my various observations about the peculiarities of the Evangelical Church, you will find everywhere the conflict between community and truth, emotion and rationality. You will read, for instance, how strong expressions of doctrinal belief foster community far more than they aid in the discovery of truth, or how pastors' sermons aim to stimulate the emotional mind before the rational mind. Evangelical Christians have extended the possibility of belonging and emotional catharsis to everyone, but to attain these benefits to their full extent, aspiring Christians are required to abandon their rationality — they must profess religious dogma with certainty, refrain from criticism of core religious ideas, and unquestionably accept dubious sources of truth. I maintain that the benefits of Christianity need not come at the expense of rational truth-seeking.

You will notice in this book that I often refer to Christianity as a society and not a community. I do this intentionally, because those words express distinct connotations. A community implies a group of independent individuals who join together on equal footing. Think of a group of next-door neighbors, or a book club. A society, on the other hand, implies a collection of individuals with different social statuses. In some cases, the Church functions as a community; in many other cases, it is more useful to think of the Church as a society, with rules and norms for traversing a moral hierarchy. This moral hierarchy rests partially upon living the life of love exemplified by Christ, but often more so upon agreeing with the pastor, saying vaguely religious things, and seeming certain in what you believe. In this book, you will find helpful tips on how to advance within the Christian society so that you too may impress your Christian peers as you share charcuterie at Wednesday night Bible study.

NOTE TO THE READER

This book will include analyses of spiritually rewarding beliefs and practices, which may hold immense personal significance to some readers. I readily understand that attempting to analyze subjective spiritual experiences is like trying to explain a good joke — it hardly ever works, and when it does, the effort tends to undermine the value of the experience in the first place. I will articulate my observations of the Church gleaned from a life within it, and while I accept that my opinions on matters of spiritually rewarding practices may come across as an attempt to undermine the value of those practices, this is not the case. An honest, rational pursuit for truth does not preclude the possibility of fulfilling subjective experiences.

Part One: Christianity in Theory

11

Christianity wades in waters that grapple with the depths of human consciousness and spirituality. These waters are mysterious, uncertain, and nuanced. Biblical texts, for instance, make many disconcerting claims. They claim that God ordered the deaths of innocent women and children, that we are steeped in sin from the moment we are born, and that it took a human sacrifice to ensure our eternal salvation. Of course, Biblical texts also contain life-affirming narratives that can positively shape the nature of morality and our pursuit of human well-being. Any honest exploration of the Christian tradition must acknowledge the difficulties and contradictions of the terrain. The Christian society should be defined by a posture of humility towards the mystery we cannot comprehend, the spirituality we cannot explain, and a text we cannot definitively interpret. Living in the faith of such a humble Christianity requires an admission that we fundamentally do not know many of life's most important questions.

Unfortunately, the Church construes core Christian concepts in ways that fail to encourage humility, truth, or honest introspection. This is evident in the way Christians often speak of three fundamental concepts: belief, faith, and doubt. These words are, of course, closely related. The person of faith is expected to believe in many things and believe in them with little doubt. Christian leaders rarely provide precise definitions for these three terms, but with enough time, their implied meanings become evident. The Church says belief is a personal conviction; I argue it is foremost a collective utility. The Church says faith is comforting; I contend it is frightening. The Church says doubt is a stumbling block; I maintain it is a necessary step towards truth.

Chapter One

The Significance of Belief

As a Christian, one is expected to believe a lot of things. Some of these things might reasonably hold bearing over one's life, such as the life of Christ and the values he taught. Many other things hold absolutely no bearing over behavior, such as the belief that Noah actually built an ark or that Mary really gave birth as a virgin. Sometimes a Christian believes because they are convinced; other times they believe because they are supposed to — the pastor says they should, or they need to so that their friends keep considering them a "true Christian." Beliefs are the rallying cries holding Christian society together, the things that tell other Christians you really are on their team. Those in the Church rarely talk about the specifics of doctrine, but you are expected to agree with them whenever they do talk about it, lest you damage your Christian reputation. Beliefs are complicated, but Christians treat them as simple. Beliefs hold the power to compel positive action, but the Church focuses on those that compel no action other than empty statements of conviction.

BELIEF AS TRIBAL

Why is it that a Christian would go out on weekends to serve the poor, or try to the best of their ability to live righteously day in and day out? I will be so bold as to say the motivating factor has nothing to do with the original sin of Adam, or the historicity of Daniel, or a creationist account of history. It has very little to do with the virgin birth of Christ, or the inerrancy of Paul, or even the existence of an afterlife. Living the life of Christ does not depend upon belief in any of these dogmas, but living the life of a Christian does. In the Christian life, you must assert a personal belief in many things that do not personally matter to you. The real power of dogmatic beliefs does not lie in their personal effects, but in their usefulness for social signaling.

To fully understand the importance of dogmatic belief for Christians, we must first understand the social significance of the Church. In the United States, Christianity offers an extraordinary social opportunity. In an adult world where people constantly struggle to find meaningful friendships, Christianity offers a welcoming group of people one wouldn't normally have the chance to befriend.[6] Christian beliefs give people something to talk about, establish a sense of shared affiliation, and provide reasons to start relationships that would otherwise never take root. Once an outsider enjoys the friendly faces, the free morning coffee, and the Father's Day car shows, they become reliant on the Church for a social network and want to delve deeper into a sense of belonging.

Whatever problems one may have with Christianity, few can deny the Church's value in helping people find meaningful community. Problems arise when the Church, which preaches a gospel of individual convictions, pressures others into beliefs not because those beliefs are personally convincing, but because they are effective for establishing community. These social pressures surely are not intentional — no pastor would say they desire a congregation bound by peer pressure — but they inevitably arise whenever groups reward dogmatic certainty. The Church will accept just about anyone into their Sunday sermons and Wednesday Bible studies, but you cannot hope to truly join the Christian society and climb upward within it unless you openly accept the correct beliefs.[7] You can live as Christ lived, love God and love your neighbor, but if you fail to state certain convictions from the script of the good Christian — or worse yet, if you actively reject them — then the group will never embrace you as much as if you had abandoned your convictions in favor of the dogma. It does not matter if you personally believe (whatever that means) in an afterlife (whatever that means), because if you do not say you believe in it then you risk creating tension in your Christian group, falling lower within the Christian society and maybe out of it altogether.

Once we recognize that dogmatic beliefs function primarily as social utilities rather than individual convictions, the Church's emphasis on such beliefs begins to make sense. People do not profess belief in something like the virgin birth of Christ because it personally changes their life; they do it because it feels good to affirm something that their community also affirms. If my colleague says they believe in the virgin birth and I say the same, what we have done is signal to each other that we reside on the same team. It's a handshake of understanding, and any shared belief will suffice to form the bond. Of course, all this forced community-building comes at a cost. By attempting to construct an artificial sense of understanding through uniform statements of belief, the Church discourages an honest exploration of individual opinions and worldviews. David Hume's "argument among friends" may lead to truth, but agreement among friends leads to stronger tribal communities.

Christians will often diminish the social dimension of belief. They will claim that doctrinal beliefs are individual convictions with supernatural consequences, but the complexities of human thought make that assertion difficult to defend.

THE INTERNAL COMPLEXITIES OF CONVICTION

According to Christianity, God will determine all our eternal fates based on our beliefs.[8] It seems important to ask: what does it mean to believe? Are beliefs collections of neurons firing at certain times in certain regions of the cerebral cortex, or are they patterns of actions involving the vocal cords and broader muscular system? If I think that I believe in the resurrection of Christ but never say it, do I believe? If I say I believe in the resurrection of Christ but do not think it as truth, what then? If, out of the 1,265 opportunities I had to state and/or think that Christ died for my sins, I thought and/or stated that I believed on 633 occasions — a slight majority — then am I thrown to eternal bliss or eternal pain?

Christians will claim that God knows the hearts of man and will decide their fates in a just and loving way. They will say that to all my discomforting questions of ambiguous belief, there exists some kind of holy algorithm the Lord will use to discern perfect and fair answers.[9] They will declare that no person can possibly comprehend the precise conditions of belief required for Heaven because humans only possess a limited earthly perspective.

Such responses miss the point. The mind does not contain a clear-cut grocery list of claims one either believes or disbelieves in.[10] Accurately and fairly extracting such a list out of the totality of human cognitive experience is not just a difficult task that humans are incapable of completing, it is an incoherent task no being could possibly accomplish. Perhaps an all-knowing God sees the hearts of man, but the hearts He finds are constantly shifting inkblots, conceptual splatter paintings impossible to definitively interpret.

To explain this point further, I will explore two false claims embedded in the Christian concept of belief:

1. Words have objective meanings.

2. We can choose our convictions.

False Claim #1: Words have objective meanings

A believer cannot be sure that the proposition they profess belief in is necessarily the same proposition that others profess belief in, because words only contain semantic value within the conscious subjects who interpret language. Consider the following proposition:

"Jesus died for my sins." The meanings of the words in this sentence will shift substantially as one matures in their knowledge of Christianity. The young and ignorant Christian's entire conception of "Jesus" might only have been shaped by what a passionate missionary told them, or the few verses of John that they happened to read.[11] "Sins," will likely refer to a set of specific actions that happen to reside at the forefront of the young believer's mind, such as the time they lied to their parents about hitting their younger sibling in the face, or when they said a 'bad word' to their friend.

Once this believer matures and learns about conventional Christian doctrine, their ideas of "Jesus" and "sins" will take on entirely new forms. The concept of Jesus will become more detailed as the believer deepens their knowledge of Scripture and experiences spiritually rewarding moments that they attribute to a personal relationship with Jesus. The idea of sin will come to include a whole new set of specific trespasses, as well as the total depravity of mankind as described by Church doctrine. It may seem like both a young and a mature Christian believe the same thing when they profess that Jesus died for their sins, but this is not the case. The two Christians hold radically different referents for the words in that sentence.[12]

What I have just described is not an exception or edge case. Every single person conceptualizes every single concept in a unique way, because every single person has experienced this world in a unique way. Objects, predicates, and categories were not given to us by the universe — humans created them, and we continue to create them. People change and mature in their understanding of concepts; for any one person to take their current conceptualization of a word or phrase and proclaim that *this* is the one true and absolute definition held by God Almighty is for them to create God in their own image. It is egoism of the highest degree.

False Claim #2: We can choose our convictions

Consider the following proposition: "Santa Claus is real." Assuming you are among the majority of Americans, you do not currently believe in the truth of that proposition, but at one point you did believe in it. Consider your childlike state of wonder and certitude in your old conviction that a jolly bearded man lives on the North Pole. Now, take a moment to try and return to that childlike state of certainty. Convince yourself once again — fully and to your core — that Santa Claus exists. Are you able to do it? The answer is almost certainly no. No matter the number of mental contortions you put yourself through and no matter the strength of your desire to change the contents of your mind, you will never return to a legitimate conviction in Santa's existence. Unless you encounter some perceptual experience that lends evidence in conflict with your current mental model of the world, your convictions about Santa will remain as they are, and there is nothing you can do about it.

Christians tend to hold an implicit assumption that people can change their internal convictions with sufficient will, but whether a proposition concerns Santa Claus or Jesus Christ, no one can consciously choose complete conviction. We cannot tell ourselves what to think in the same we cannot tell a painting to change its colors. For the painting's colors to change, an artist must apply new paint; for an individual's convictions to change, experience must recolor the canvas of their worldview. This reality poses a fundamental problem for the Christian ideas of divine grace and eternal salvation, which rely upon the principle that people can will their convictions into alignment with the doctrines required for Heaven. Under this idea, anyone can accept the statements necessary for eternal life so long as they possess the requisite desire to follow the ways of God. A good Christian attempts to replace doubt with conviction, but just as nobody can choose when they understand a riddle or get a joke, no one can choose when they are fully convinced of any religious belief.

Humans bear many layers, many voices that speak different truths. We must recognize that thought is not so one-dimensional. On many important topics, people reside in an uncomfortable limbo between belief and disbelief. The idea of a heavenly afterlife may exist as a certain reality at the forefront of one's mind while simultaneously existing as utter nonsense deep within the psyche, yelling behind all the walls one chooses to put up around the inconvenient thought. As long as someone does not pause to think too deeply, we say they believe, yet if they delve deeper into their mind, then they doubt. This mental state of contradictory intuitions — which absolutely exists in many people — precludes any possibility of complete internal conviction. We do not control everything that occurs in our minds, and we must accept the impossibility of forcing all our thoughts into alignment with doctrine.[13]

* * *

Our mental models of the world follow no simple organizing principle. We can try to make sense of each other's worldviews through the language of belief and disbelief, though such attempts are inevitably lossy — they reduce our complex mental models to binary statements either affirming or denying the truth of certain claims, claims with words that are themselves lossy representations of more complex ideas. While many seem to think of the mind as a book with neatly spelled out thoughts and beliefs, mental experience does not support this claim. People believe all sorts of things that they have never considered in language. For instance, I have long held a strong conviction that purple flying unicorns do not exist, but, before this very moment, I never thought to extract this belief out of my worldview. This is to say, we *discover* our beliefs, which arise out of a mental model of the world shaped by factors outside our control, and we *represent* our beliefs through words that hold different meanings to different people.

Unfortunately, Christians claim to know Heaven's immigration policy, and they say that this policy requires the internal acceptance of certain propositions. No room exists for the complexities of mental models or verbal representations. If someone does not, for instance, think that Jesus Christ died for their sins, then the Church says they will burn in a literal Hell for a literal eternity. To the Church, it does not matter that nobody can choose to internalize complete conviction in an arbitrary claim; it does not matter that everyone holds different conceptions of Jesus, sins, or the vague concept of an atoning human sacrifice. None of reality's inconveniences matter — Christians must simply agree with dogmatic statements because there always exists a gun to their head threatening Hell if they ever change their minds. Everyone should plainly see that such a state of affairs is neither healthy nor conducive to truth-seeking. Rather than encouraging honest intro- spection, Christian society frowns upon those who depart from the sentences deemed necessary for Heav- en. This entire framework of eternal life based on in- ternal convictions falls apart once we understand that words have no objective meaning and we cannot choose our convictions, but it should not take these realizations to abandon the eminently unhealthy idea that we all must think certain thoughts in order to be given everlasting happiness.

In this section, I hope to have communicated three positions. First, that the contents of the mind cannot possibly serve as a just entry pass into an afterlife. Second, that thinking of belief as possessing such dire metaphysical consequences is counterproductive to an honest exploration of what we actually think. Third, that our thoughts and opinions are often difficult to unearth and clearly communicate to others. In the next section, I will explore how beliefs become more com- prehensible when conceptualized in terms of external action rather than internal conviction.

BELIEF AS ACTION

If we think that beliefs should define a person in some knowable way, then beliefs cannot exist only as thoughts unknown to the outside world. Societies ultimately care about how others act, not how they think. Framing belief in terms of behavioral patterns rather than thought patterns makes the concept available for a social analysis.

The extent to which actions should define belief has long been a matter of theological debate. Martin Luther — a strong advocate of the view that belief is solely an internal affair — famously despised the biblical book of James, which proclaims that "faith without works is dead." Luther rants here:

> "We should throw the epistle of James out of this school, for it doesn't amount to much. ... I maintain that some Jew wrote it who probably heard about Christian people but never encountered any. Since he heard that Christians place great weight on faith in Christ, he thought, 'Wait a moment! I'll oppose them and urge works alone.' This he did."[14]

The book of James, which remains in the Protestant canon despite Luther's disdain for it, serves as evidence that even authors of the Bible recognized the apparent truth that thoughts and convictions do not amount to anything unless they manifest in action.

The modern Church does not deny that actions serve as a key component of belief, but it asks for more than just action. Christian society encourages a complete unity of thought, feeling, and behavior all in alignment with doctrine, though this is not possible or even desirable. It is not possible because of mental complexities (as explained in the previous section), and it is not desirable because it means Christians would have to suppress inconvenient thoughts that might nonetheless be useful in the pursuit of truth.

Instead of framing action as just one among many variables in a complex definition of belief, I argue that we should instead think of action as the sole determinant of belief. A behavioral understanding of belief leaves space for the complexities of our roaming thoughts and allows the internal exploration of contrarian ideas. Whatever doubts I may hold in the existence of God, if I say that I believe in God and act as though God exists, then I legitimately believe in God from society's frame of reference. The thoughts we choose to act upon define our identity and our beliefs within a society.

A purely behavioral definition of belief is not particularly intuitive, because people very often use the words "belief" and "conviction" synonymously. Under my framing, these two words hold different meanings. "Conviction" refers to internal mental activity, while "belief" refers only to acts that others may observe. Beliefs that manifest through the act of statement alone are real and legitimate beliefs, but I argue that such statement-only beliefs are not particularly meaningful.

* * *

About a month ago, I became completely convinced in the truth of two claims. The first claim: "People should love their enemies." The second claim: "Everyone with brown hair possesses a harmless, invisible, and subatomic elf named Igor living in their small intestine." My conviction in the moral imperative to love one's enemies has had a profound impact on my behavior. Over the past month, I have been kinder to those who wrong me, I have begun regularly inviting my grouchy next-door neighbor over for dinner, and I have stopped gossiping with co-workers about my annoying boss. On the other hand, my belief in Igor the intestinal elf has not had the same impact. Other than when I first told my friends and family about Igor, the conviction has had no effect whatsoever on my behavior. Some friends and family did not even believe me when I told them my thoughts about Igor, but I could think of no action to provide proof of my belief outside of simply repeating my statement of conviction.[15]

Usually, people look for more than just a statement to determine if they think someone truly believes a claim. If I said to my friends, "I believe people should love their enemies," then proceeded to swiftly murder all my enemies out of spite, my friends would likely conclude that I did not actually believe in what I had stated. Put generally, people will reason that if someone truly believes in the truth of a claim, then they will behave according to a set of actions associated with that claim. If someone does not behave according to that set of actions whatsoever, then we would say that this person does not truly believe in the associated claim. A person can say that they love their enemies despite actually hating them; likewise, someone can say that they hate their enemies despite actually loving them. Statement of belief does not always entail actual belief.

I should wonder, then: what set of actions does society expect me to adhere to if I truly accept the existence of Igor the harmless, invisible, subatomic elf? For me to believe in this dogma, there is no act I could reasonably take other than to simply state that I believe in it — no other behavioral change flows from my strange conviction in the existence of Igor.[16] Because the set of actions associated with the claim of loving one's enemies is more significant than the set of actions associated with the claim of subatomic elves, we can say that belief in the former is more *meaningful* than belief in the latter. This is to say, beliefs that reasonably manifest in action outside of mere statement are more meaningful than beliefs that do not.

In sum, people believe in things within a society by expressing their convictions through actions. Many beliefs that bear great tribal importance within the Christian society are akin to the belief in Igor the elf. They do not reasonably manifest in meaningful action.

BELIEF IN HISTORICAL MIRACLES

A pastor once told me that Christians should believe in the prophecies and historicity of the biblical book of Daniel. I thought this a rather bold claim. The book was written in three different languages and three different narrative tenses, indicating that the work was not penned by a historical Daniel as Christians often claim.[17] It contains multiple deviations from known historical facts, and there is near universal consensus among scholars that the book was written nearly 400 years after the events described within it.[18] The book of

Daniel, by any reasonable standard, should not be treated as a historical account.

Nothing in this fact takes away from the meaning or applicability of Daniel, because the value of a story does not depend upon its reality. All Christians know this, unless they find no value in a fictional figure like the Good Samaritan because he is 'simply' a character in a story. In countless sermons, I have seen pastors confidently assert the historical occurrence of biblical stories even though these assertions do nothing to affect the applicability of their messages.[19] These pastors say that Christians should believe in the complete historicity of Genesis, Joshua, Judges, Chronicles, or any number of other books that clearly contain non-historical stories. Belief in the historicity of these books is not only unreasonable, it is nearly meaningless.

We have already established that for a belief claim to be meaningful it must be actionable in some significant way. We should ask ourselves: how does one act as though Daniel is historical? As with any belief, the historicity of Daniel can compel significant action in certain edge cases. Maybe you are an obsessed archeologist who spends years searching for the fabled lion's den, or perhaps you are a daring missionary who puts themselves in great danger on the assurance that God will save you just as He saved Daniel's friends from the furnace flames. Of course, such acts of meaningful belief in Daniel's historicity are not at all common, nor are they necessary for society to accept the belief as legitimate. For the overwhelming majority of Christians, belief in the historicity of Daniel amounts to nothing more than the act of saying aloud to a friend, "I believe Daniel existed." What else could one reasonably do? For most historical claims, and many other theological claims, to believe means nothing more than to say you believe.[20]

Presumably, evangelists and apologists demand belief in historical concepts such as a historical Daniel or a 6,000-year-old earth not because those facts in themselves compel action, but because these claims serve as part of a larger persuasion leading to a meaningful belief in Jesus Christ. Here goes the thinking: if someone becomes convinced in the historicity of miraculous biblical stories, then they will become convinced in the existence of the Christian God. This line of argument is completely backwards. Christians do not believe in God because of miracles; they believe in miracles because they already believe in God.

Historical miracles do not lead to belief in God

When someone testifies about the occurrence of some miracle, they are really making two claims: 1) some extraordinary event occurred, and 2) the cause of that event was a supernatural power. Take this famous miraculous claim from Genesis:

> "And after seven days the waters of the flood came on the earth. ... [God] blotted out every living thing that was on the face of the ground, human beings and animals and creeping things and birds of the air; they were blotted out from the earth. Only Noah was left and those with him in the ark." (Genesis 7:10, 23; NRSVue)

Among other things, this passage claims that 1) a deadly flood covered the earth, and 2) the Hebrew God caused the deadly flood. The claim that makes this miracle *meaningful* is the assertion of God's existence in the second claim. A large flood thousands of years ago does not compel action in the modern reader, but God's existence does. The question then remains: if we accept that the events from the first claim actually occurred, does that necessarily lead us to accept the assertion of God's existence made in the second claim? The answer is clearly no. Whether an extraordinary occurrence of events is interpreted to have been caused by God or by physics depends entirely on the predisposition of the person hearing the story. I may accept that the earth flooded thousands of years ago while rejecting the possibility that a supernatural being caused the flood.[21] Humans are only capable of directly observing events; we cannot directly observe the metaphysical causes of events.[22] Conclusions as to the causes of events are judgments that we make *after* having observed something. Meaning is not embedded within occurrences; it is created by humans and shaped by our biases.

Of course, some extraordinary occurrences in the Bible strongly suggest a divine cause. If I accepted as historical fact that 2,500 years ago a hand appeared out of thin air, wrote a Hebrew phrase on the wall of King Belshazzar's palace, and that a religious Hebrew man named Daniel correctly interpreted the writing as a prophecy that Darius the Mede would soon conquer the Babylonian Empire, then I would be hard pressed to find a reasonable cause for these events other than the actual existence of Daniel's God.[23] The pertinent question then remains: what could have led me to believe that these events occurred? Physical evidence could not be the reason, as none exists. Historical rigor could not be the reason, as reliable sources tell us that both King Belshazzar and Darius the Mede either did not exist or were not who the narrative claims they are.[24] Alignment with personal experience likewise offers no reason for belief, since nothing in my experience leads me to expect hands suddenly appearing out of thin air.[25] Without pre-existing belief in the kind of God who could cause the miracles of the Bible, there is no reason to believe in the miracles of the Bible.

People do not begin praying to God or following Jesus because they become convinced in the historical existence of Daniel or Noah. Strange and unactionable historical convictions arise *after* someone has already joined the Christian group. Maybe I am wrong, and it really is the case that people's commitment to the teachings of Jesus hinges upon the actual existence of floating hands or giant arks. If this is the case, then I do not know what to tell these people other than that they have entirely missed the point of following Christ.

* * *

A kind of question that never ceases to be amusing, and that often gets asked by children, is the inquisitive "what if?" What if humans had three legs? What if bears could fly? What if water fountains shot out string cheese instead of water?! Very often, firm answers to these kinds of questions are impossible, and the only appropriate response is some form of the statement, "that would be cool, I guess." Instead, children ask these questions not because they want answers, but because they can lead to fun conversation and social bonding. Listening to Christians repeatedly assert the historicity of miraculous events is like hearing children ask each other what-ifs. "What if Daniel really existed, or David really slew Goliath?!" What answer can one give, other than to say, "that would be cool, I guess? No deeper meaning or action reasonably flows from these statements of historicity.

Biblical stories hold immense opportunities for study and reflection. They may well be useful "for teaching, for reproof, for correction, and for training in righteousness." (2 Timothy 3:16, NRSVue) None of these benefits, however, arise from the actual occurrence of the events these stories describe.

CONCLUSION

A person cannot choose to be convinced of something. If, after much thought and consideration, I do not think the physical resurrection of Christ occurred, then I must lie to myself and to others in order to maintain my status within Christian society. And yet, with this lie, I do legitimately believe in all functional capacities. People only know the person we present, and that is who we are within a society. If I say I believe in Christ's resurrection then I believe in Christ's resurrection, even if I do not legitimately think it occurred. This paradox only manages to persist because Christian society does not expect dogmatic convictions to substantially alter anyone's behavior.[26] If I lie by professing belief in dogma that I do not think is true, no one could call my bluff because the only indication of belief stems from the bluff itself. Following the way of Jesus does not, in actuality, depend upon the reality of Christ's resurrection, or the historicity of Daniel, or any of the many doctrines I have already mentioned, yet Christians have made verbal acceptance of these ideas necessary for full acceptance into the group.

I understand the appeal of believing in unfalsifiable doctrine. I know the allure of viewing oneself as part of a grand biblical history, or some cosmic theological framework. However, I am convinced that true behavioral change is best achieved within communities prioritizing the pursuit of truth over certainty in doctrine, even doctrine as poetically convenient as that which is commonly preached. All too often, Christians fail to recognize that the true value of belief rests in *story* rather than history, in *doing* rather than dogma. Beliefs will not determine whether we live a fulfilling afterlife in Heaven, but we can choose to let them determine whether we live a fulfilling life on this earth.

To fit in the Christian society, believe in things, but do not think about them.

Chapter Two

The Concept of Faith

Very often, people use "faith" and "belief" to mean exactly the same thing: personal conviction.[27] However, most Christians will intuitively recognize that faith carries some special connotations not carried by belief. Christians typically use faith to imply a kind of divine and fearless certainty, though I will argue that this conception of faith is neither helpful nor biblical. Christians often leverage faith as a powerful response to difficult questions, though I will contend that such responses are neither profound nor coherent. Faith *could* be profound; it could be coherent and helpful and nuanced and biblical, but such an improved conception of faith is not the one Christian society has chosen to reward.

FAITH AS AN ANSWER TO HARD QUESTIONS

I could give endless examples of how Christians use faith as an answer to hard questions. Why do some believe in the rapture and apocalyptic end times with such detail?[28] "Faith," the good Christian will say. What of eternal life and the problem of God sending innocent people to Hell? Faith, of course. How about the genocide of the Canaanites described in Joshua, the historicity of the creation myth, or the second coming of Christ? Faith, faith, and a lot of faith. Instead of saying, "I don't know," the good Christian appeals to faith. It is worth exploring why Christians tend to rely on faith rather than belief when those two words ostensibly mean the same thing.

Take two people who make the following claims:

Bob: **I have faith** that I will live forever.

Larry: **I believe** that I will live forever.

Strictly speaking, these two sentences mean the same thing — both the speakers purport to hold a conviction in the reality of an eternal life. However, consider what happens once you ask Bob and Larry to explain *why* they hold their convictions.

Bob: I am convinced because **I have faith**.

Larry: I am convinced because **I believe**.

Bob's explanation sounds like a coherent thought that someone might actually state, while Larry's sounds like a circular response someone might provide when they can think of no good justification for their conviction. This should seem strange to us, since "faith" and "belief" are often synonymous. Both Bob's and Larry's responses should be equally circular and incoherent, but for whatever reason, "faith" may be used to mean both "conviction" and "a valid reason for conviction."

One possible reason for this strangeness could be that belief only points inwards towards oneself, whereas faith points outwards to a higher power. When Bob claims to have faith, he implies that he has faith *in* someone or something external. Larry cannot say the same by merely appealing to belief, which implies that the idea arose only out of himself and not from some outside authority.

This simple observation about the difference in *effectiveness* between the two words does not actually point to any difference in *substance*. They are still perfectly interchangeable within the Church — in every instance that I use the word "belief," I could just as easily use the phrasing of "faith." While it may seem like "faith" offers ideas a kind of special legitimacy from an external force, this is just an illusion. If you justify a personal conviction by using the word "belief," then no one will take you seriously. But if you simply communicate the idea with the phrasing of "faith," then, like a spell, you will see your ideas command respect in society.

To be clear, faith can reasonably mean something deeper than simply "conviction," and in future sections I will argue that faith holds great potential for describing the deeper challenges of human experience. That said, common Christian parlance does not abide by the nuanced definition I will later advocate for. In its common usage within the Church, "faith" simply means "strong conviction;" as such, no one should be able to use faith as a justification for convictions.[29] The statement, "I am convinced because I have faith," is equivalent to the statement, "I am convinced because I am convinced" — it is stubbornness masquerading as strength.[30] Instead of ever conceding to ignorance or engaging in the difficult introspection that could uncover the true roots of belief, Christians will all-too-often take the easy way out when asked to justify their convictions. They will provide the illusion of a response in "faith." This shield of faith has become far too protective for Christians; it has shielded them from the need to learn more about the beliefs they purport to hold.

Serious inquiry cannot begin until one admits to a level of ignorance. For a rational pursuit of truth, "I don't know" is the start of a journey. The answer of faith, on the other hand, ends any possibility of further investigation. It signals at least two things about the believer: they do not know any good reason for believing what they believe, and they have no intention of changing their belief. This is the antithesis of rational thinking, and it is not the posture of someone whose goal is truth.

Within the Christian society, the person who has an answer — even one as banal as faith — often sits higher in the minds of other Christians than the one who admits to their human ignorance.

FAITH AS CERTAINTY

When the topic of faith appears, many Christians will quickly turn to Hebrews 11:1, which seems to offer a very clear definition:

> "Now faith is the assurance of things hoped for, the conviction of things not seen." (NRSVue)

The author of Hebrews goes on to outline several Biblical 'knights of faith' whom the Church commends, such as Abel, Abraham, and Moses. It would seem, then, that the book of Hebrews presents a rather straightforward message: the more sure and certain we are, the more faithful and heroic we become. This is the end of the matter for most discussion in the Church. However, if we take Hebrews' definition of faith at face value, then we find that actions of assuredness and conviction are commendable in some instances just as they are condemnable in others.

I might very easily hope for any number of selfish things, from the election of my favored political candidate to the swift destruction of my enemies. Is it good that I am always assured of things I hope for? I also don't see a lot of things. God is one of them, but so is a purple flying unicorn. Should I really have conviction in everything I do not see? Christians do not commend Abraham simply because he had faith by the definition of Hebrews, they commend him because he possessed the kind of faith that allowed him to follow a righteous path despite his fear and uncertainty. Hebrews 11 provides only the broadest imaginable conception of faith, one that just isn't very useful when attempting to apply normative value to the concept.

Much ambiguity surrounds the meaning of faith within the Church because no one discusses its definition beyond Hebrews 11:1. The standard Christian line of thinking goes something along the lines of, "faith is a good thing, faith means certainty, so I should be certain in order to be good." I find this attitude naive and discouraging. It makes no attempt to reconcile the barebones definition of faith in Hebrews with the uncertain complexity contained in every single book of the biblical canon. A self-proclaimed follower of God might feel the need to exude certainty in the basic existence of a God (whatever that might mean), but beyond this core assurance in what Christians hope for, there remains much for the knight of faith to doubt.

FAITH AS THE OPPOSITE OF FEAR

Within the Church, I repeatedly come across the idea that faith is the antidote to fear. This sentiment can be found everywhere in feel-good Christian dialogue. For example:

> "It's important to know that fear does not come from God. In fact, God wants us to walk by faith, while Satan wants us to walk in fear."[31]

> "Faith and fear cannot exist together."[32]

> "Faith is a constant command in the scriptures, and it's opposed to the feelings of dread and fear. Of course, the greatest command in the

44

Bible is do not be afraid, do not worry, do not
fear. Faith is the opposite of fear. Faith is the
thing that fosters joy, possibilities, and hope,
and it cultivates the calling of God in your
life."[33]

The Bible does not paint such a straightforward
picture of faith and fear. It is true that, in some instances, the Bible depicts faith as something antithetical to
fear. For one such instance, we can look to the story of
Jesus calling Peter to walk on water. In this story, Peter
successfully walks on water for a moment, but soon
becomes afraid of the strong winds and sinks. Jesus
chastises him, saying, "You of little faith, why did you
doubt?" (Matthew 14:31b, NRSVue). Rather clearly,
Jesus uses the word "faith" in this story to mean the
opposite of fear and doubt. The fact of the matter,
however, is that the Bible does not provide a unified
definition of faith. In many other Biblical passages, the
call to faith *creates* fear.

Consider when God commands Abraham to kill
his only son or Moses to confront Pharaoh. Recall that
God calls on Gideon to lead his 300 men against thousands, and Esther to approach her king unannounced.[34]
Christianity's perfect person, Jesus Christ, sweats blood
at Gethsemane in dread of his looming torture. Would
any of us chastise Jesus for a lack of faith?[35] Fear and

trembling accompany many paradigmatic instances of faith in the Bible, and necessarily so. As it happens, going against the grain of society to boldly follow a personal conviction tends to be a rather uncomfortable, frightening endeavor.[36]

The idea of faith meaning an absence of fear relies on an understanding of belief as meaning an absolute conviction. Insofar as someone has completely resigned themselves to a hopeful idea, then faith reasonably functions as the perfect opposite of fear; however, if belief does not entail absolute conviction and we accept that doubt inevitably exists in the mind of anyone with worthwhile beliefs, then we must allow faith and fear to coexist.

Currently, the Church largely treats faith as a passive feeling that helps believers cope with fear, though many stories of the Bible seem to paint a different picture, one that presents faith as an internal activity challenging believers to enter frightening waters. That feeling of divine peace and perfect hope, which Christians commonly call faith, certainly seems a good and desirable thing, though I think we discount the profound concept of faith by so broadly utilizing it to describe anything good, godly, and righteous. No nuance and very little truth can be found in the unrealistic call to let faith erase fear.

CONCLUSION

Within the Christian lexicon, there exists many words with no precise meaning beyond the vaguely positive emotions they stir. I can speak effusively of God's goodness, grace, love, patience, power, salvation, holiness, grace, compassion, and so on, all to the nodding approval of my Christian peers. If you ask a theologian what these words mean, they will provide detailed, distinct, and nuanced definitions, but if you observe what actually occurs in the mind of the average Christian nodding along, you will find that the words meld together into a singular gelatinous glob of good feeling. "Faith" has become one such faded word within the Church.

Christians can continue to use "faith" as a quick and easy answer to fear or uncertainty, though in doing so, they surely cheapen a concept with such rich potential for describing the paradox and mystery that is our innermost selves. A deeper understanding of faith demands careful and nuanced language; Christian society rewards vaguely uplifting platitudes instead.

To fit in the Christian society, define "faith" as "good" and liberally utilize it as the antidote to anything "bad."

Chapter Three

That Disease Called Doubt

Mr. Christian: Wow, that was a great sermon on doubt today. I wonder if there is anything that you doubt?

Me: Well, to be honest, I'm not so sure that I buy the virgin birth of Jesus. I just don't think it makes any sense.

Mr. Christian: Thanks so much for sharing that with me. May I pray for you about this doubts?

From the outside looking in, it seems quite odd that Christians consider prayer an appropriate response to religious doubt. Presumably, the well-meaning Christian in the above example thinks that I am straying away from a life-bringing truth, and they want me to return to the better path. They probably think I am torn up over my doubt, perplexed and in despair, so they offer a prayer of comfort. I do not doubt that such prayers come from places of good intention, yet I can think of few acts more patronizing than praying for a peer to overcome wholly reasonable doubts.

48

Within the Church, doubt is something to be avoided. To doubt means to become less certain and therefore less faithful. In any other context, society usually sees doubt and skepticism as necessary for the discovery of truth; not so in the Christian society, where truth is given, not discovered. In such a society, doubt is a disease for God to cure.

DOUBT AS A PARTNER TO FAITH

Before critiquing the Church's approach to doubt, I want to first discuss the concept of doubt in the context of belief and faith.

Doubt can be defined as a thought or feeling of uncertainty in the truth of a claim. Belief, as it is commonly thought of within the Church, is just the opposite: a thought or a feeling of assurance in the truth a claim. In one moment, I might hold complete assurance in the idea that Jesus will return to earth by descending from the clouds, while at some other moment I might doubt by thinking the second coming improbable. Insofar as belief is an internal conviction, I cannot fully believe in the second coming of Christ while simultaneously holding doubt in its truth; however, if we think of belief as action, then it is possible to possess internal dissent from the belief claims we express through behavior. I may doubt that Christ will return again, but if I continually make statements indicating that I think he will return and act in ways that prepare for the looming end of the world, then I fully and legitimately believe in the second coming of Christ under an behavioral definition of belief. Internal doubt and external belief very often coexist.

"Faith" sometimes serves as an exact synonym for "belief," though not always. For instance, most would agree that there is a slight difference in meaning between "living a life of belief" and "living a life of faith." Living a life of belief simply means that one goes about life accepting certain things to be true, while living a life of faith implies that one goes about life accepting certain things to be true *despite* personal difficulties, struggles, or doubts. In this sense, faith is the force of will that allows one to continue believing in a claim through action despite possessing internal uncertainty in the truth of that claim. Such faith cannot exist without doubt.

When discussing faith in this context, we should keep a few points in mind.

1. We must take care not to tint the concept of faith with judgments of right or wrong. Faith, according to the definition I am advocating for, is not inherently good or evil — it is simply a descriptor for the act of

behaviorally expressing certain beliefs despite intellectually holding doubt in the truth of those beliefs. Altruistic saints and terroristic extremists might both possess true and legitimate faith. Whether I think someone should or should not live a life of faith depends entirely on the belief claims they plan to act in service of.

2. This definition of faith means that living according to faith is not particularly special and not necessarily religious. This morning, I expressed doubt as to whether my refrigerator contained any milk, yet I nonetheless poured myself a full bowl of cereal based on the belief that the refrigerator did contain milk. I would say that I possessed faith in the existence of milk in my refrigerator.[37]

3. There are at least two general ways in which someone may live by faith: someone may act according to a belief by suppressing and ignoring the voices of doubt within them, or they act according to a belief while honestly accepting and exploring those voices of doubt. I argue that everyone should want to live by the latter kind of faith.

Many within the Church would not find my proposed relationship between faith and doubt so objectionable. After all, many a sermon extols the virtues of doubting and encourages Christians to openly share their doubts with their church-going peers. That said, the Church encourages this sharing of doubts not so that people may freely consider the truth of dogma, but so that they might recognize a fault in their thinking. Teachings on doubt imply that if a Christian is truly righteous, then their doubts in God-given doctrine will eventually recede. For instance, if I doubt in the resurrection of Christ, the Church would surely welcome the expression of my doubt. They would expect me to take time to pray, study the Word, and wrestle with my doubts before faithfully arriving at a more certain conviction that Christ did, in fact, rise from the dead. Doubt poses no hindrance at all to one's climb within the Christian society so long as the good Christian takes care to never change their beliefs from the dogma initially held. I find that a wrestling match holds little value when the victor is fixed from the outset.[38] We should not think of doubt as a stumbling block to righteous living but rather as a practice that is necessary for discovering truth and living a life of faith.

FACTS AND VALUES

I maintain that the acknowledgment and expression of doubts always leads to greater truth and greater personal well-being, regardless of what those doubts concern. Acknowledging and expressing doubts may be healthy, but it is not always easy, and I do not want to diminish the immense fear or discomfort that can accompany the act of doubting personally meaningful beliefs. That said, many beliefs within Christianity are not personally meaningful, and while the Church has made doubt in these inconsequential dogmas *socially* difficult, we should not pretend that such doubts are *personally* difficult.

I see two broad types of belief claims that Christians advocate for — fact claims and value claims. The belief that some event occurred or will occur is categorically different from the belief that one ought to follow some moral maxim. We can usually count on beliefs regarding matters of moral values to be meaningful, because moral values directly relate to the behavior of individuals. Beliefs regarding matters of fact can sometimes lead to behavioral change, but, as already discussed, the Church does not expect many such beliefs to lead to any action beyond mere statement.[39]

Christian society makes little distinction between the act of doubting Christian value claims and the act of doubting Christian fact claims — both kinds of doubt are akin to a sickness requiring remedy. This is not reasonable.

Is our doubt in the inerrancy of scripture supposed to stop us from giving to the poor, the widows, and the

orphans? Are we to hate our neighbors and our enemies because we find the virgin birth of Christ confusing? Dogmatic ideas within the Church often hold no
relation to moral values, yet the Church places both
under the broad umbrella of "belief" and socially dis-
advantages those who doubt in any of the varied ideas
within that umbrella. I argue that the realm of appropriate Christian debate should expand to incorporate
doctrinal topics commonly thought of as taboo, because
Christians can doubt a vast number of 'necessary'
dogma without altering their Christian morals.

Value Claims	Fact Claims
People should love their neighbors as themselves	Jesus of Nazareth rose from the dead
Honesty is the best policy	Moses wrote the Pentateuch
People who don't return shopping carts are jerks	I will financially prosper because of my faith

Empirical evidence supports the claim that dogmatic beliefs hold no relation to values. Political scientists Robert Putnam and David Campbell collected
extensive survey data on American Christians between
2006 and 2007. They found that American Christians

were significantly more generous and altruistic than their secular peers — they gave more to charity, expressed greater attitudes of neighborly helpfulness, etc. — however, these patterns of altruism were completely unrelated to belief or disbelief in Christian dogma. It did not matter whether someone prayed outside of religious services or thoroughly believed that eternal life awaited them after death — neighborliness depended solely upon social interaction within a religious community. To quote the authors directly, "The real impact of religiosity on niceness or good neighborliness, it seems, comes through chatting with friends after service or joining a Bible study group, not from listening to the sermon or fervently believing in God."[40]

Putnam and Campbell's research indicates that no relationship exists between the 'Christian lifestyle' and Christian dogmas. By continuously asserting the opposite and socially penalizing those who express doctrinal doubts, the Church misses an opportunity to allow more people into a meaningful sense of belonging. Without sacrificing much other than pride, Christian society could choose to alter its moral hierarchy in a way that rewards those who exude the love of Christ without regard for their opinions concerning irrelevant dogma.[41]

CONCLUSION

We do not need dogmatic certainty to have close friendships or positive morals. Communities can remain enjoyable and fulfilling even as they encourage honest discussions of doubts that are unobstructed by pressures towards any one conclusion. The Church cannot pretend to support truth or vulnerability when its members must risk social penalties to voice their opinions. As it stands, doubts within the Church are challenges to be overcome, not ideas to be seriously wrestled with. The Christian who never doubts certainly sits high within Christian society, though perhaps higher still stand those who doubted in despair before triumphantly arriving back exactly where they started.

To fit in the Christian society, never express a doubt unless you are willing to repent of it.

Part Two: Christianity in Practice

Sitting around a table inside a small room in the church annex, my high school friends and I share in fellowship at our weekly Wednesday night Bible study. Leading the group is an adult volunteer, who ends his prepared message with the following call for reflection:

> "Satan can appear in many areas of our lives, and we should be aware of the spiritual warfare that surrounds us every day. Now, let's go around and share some prayer requests."

Two theological concepts arose in a single sentence: Satan and spiritual warfare. I sit with my friends wondering what the leader could have meant. Did he mean an actual supernatural being named "Satan" exists? Is he saying a literal spiritual war is happening around us, full of invisible angels and demons? Perhaps he meant something far more symbolic. After all, "Satan" literally means "adversary," and we can reasonably think of evil as a symbolic adversary to the way of God. The concept of spiritual warfare likewise functions perfectly well as a purely symbolic representation of love working against hate. I would be comfortable using the language of Satan and spiritual warfare despite not believing in a celestial realm because I understand the power of imagery and anthropomorphism; however, it seems like this church group very often talks about Satan and spiritual warfare in ways that imply they actually believe in the existence of super-natural beings.

As my thoughts swirl, the conversation quickly moves on. Any opportunity I had to pin down exactly what was meant by such vague language goes passing. In any case, it would have been awkward to interrupt the spiritual atmosphere of the group with such a rational question. We continue with the Bible study by sharing prayer requests, feeling guilty for not reading the Bible enough, and engaging in friendly chit-chat.

* * *

Observe the Christian society intently and you will notice the deftness with which Church leaders and Church goers spread their doctrine, stating them in passing with complete certainty and leaving no space for dissent. An average Christian, uninformed in aca-demic Biblical interpretation, will often get pushed along by the steady flow of questionable doctrine that undergirds the Christian dialogue. Few church leaders will say on their own accord, "Satan really exists as a supernatural being and you should agree;" rather, people will simply act as though this is what everyone thinks. Such a society of unexplored ideas only manag-es to persist because 1) these ideas do not meaningfully relate to action (as discussed in Part One), and 2) spiritually stimulating rituals, not doctrines, serve as the real cohesive glue behind the Christian society.

To the common Christian, it does not matter what the lyrics of the worship music say, only that they are vaguely Christian and the accompanying chord progression stirs emotion. To most committed churchgoers, it is of little importance that not a single person at a Bible study holds deep academic understanding of the Bible, because the value of such a ritual comes from meeting with friends and sharing life's difficulties. I wholeheartedly enjoy the emotional, feel-good aspects of the Christian faith; however, I see an excess of Christians who consistently value spirituality over study and emotion over reason. In my experience, it eventually became exhausting continually feeling obligated to go along with statements I disagreed with because those statements emotionally resonated with too many people in my Christian circle.

In Part One, I explored how the Church construes core religious ideas in ways that promote stronger tribal cohesion. I now aim to demonstrate how these misguided conceptions of belief, faith, and doubt tangibly manifest in the routine exercise of Christianity. The following chapters of this book contain distinct essays exploring various elements in the script a good Christian must adhere to.

Chapter Four

Small Group Bible Study

At every Evangelical Bible study I have attended, someone always ends up asking the same basic question: "how does this lesson apply to your life?" Most times I also get asked about how I sinned this past week, or what I did that was righteous. It is always about me, how *I* sinned, how *I* can do better. This is because Bible study is not really about studying the Bible; it is about studying ourselves.

This observation holds no inherent judgment. Studying ourselves with true vulnerability might be one of the most important endeavors we can undertake, and the Church's promotion of such introspection can only be praised — however, the couching of such introspection within a routine of biblical study cheapens both the introspection and the biblical study. There exists in many small groups an awkward dance between two irrelevant goals: the academic study of a thousand-year-old text, and the creation of meaningful friendships based in self-improvement.

Let me lay out a standard small group ritual from my experience. I would spend the first fifteen minutes or-so eating food and talking with my friends. At some point we all sat down, prayed, and then the group leader would read a few Bible verses, asking us some comprehension questions along the way. The leader then read from prepared Bible study pamphlet to make a deft thematic transition into the same questions about personal development we got asked every week. After everyone shared ways they sinned and ways to improve (or made up ways they sinned and ways to improve), we closed with prayer requests and I got back to chatting with my friends and eating food.

The two essential components of this ritual (the parts that make a Christian small group *Christian*) are 1) discussion of biblical passages and 2) discussion of sin and repentance. These two components often manifest in questions of biblical comprehension and questions of personal improvement.

BIBLICAL COMPREHENSION

Comprehension questions generally take the form of Sunday school questions with Sunday school answers; that is to say, trivial questions with self-evident answers. They are the kinds of questions that do not make you consider anything other than whether you want to waste your breath giving the obviously 'correct' answer everyone already knows. Answering one of these comprehension questions usually involves re-reading a piece of scripture that the small group leader stated just moments ago — this small group leader is very often just a fellow Christian peer who the group tasked with delivering a short message prepared by the pastor. As an example:

> **Leader:** Dylan, can you please read the passage for the group?
>
> **Me:** Sure, Matthew 4:41. "The disciples were terrified and asked each other, 'Who is this? Even the wind and the waves obey him!'"
>
> **Leader:** Thank you Dylan. So everyone, how were the disciples feeling?
>
> **Group:** *awkward silence*
>
> **Me:** ...they were feeling terrified.
>
> **Leader:** Exactly! That's right!

To say the least, these questions do not exactly push the boundaries of critical thought. As is usually the case, finding the right question poses a far greater challenge than finding the right answer. Small groups often only ask comprehension questions because such questions do not require any substantive biblical knowledge in history, anthropology, or linguistics, which no one in the group possesses.

If the purpose of Christian small groups is the study of biblical texts, then we must wonder why Christians think they can accomplish this goal when no one in the small group knows anything more than the next guy about the Bible. At most Bible studies, nobody has put in the time and study that would be necessary to offer anything meaningful beyond what everyone already plainly sees, or what anyone could quickly read in the study pamphlet prepared by the pastor. Christians should stop trying to study the Bible at Bible studies and just accept the time for what it is: a gathering of friends. They should have a good time, share openly about their lives, and save the Bible study for another time when someone knowledgeable can provide informed analysis. Unfortunately, that time usually never comes, and most Christians never get to ask critical questions about the book that supposedly shapes their lives.

PERSONAL IMPROVEMENT

After the shallow comprehension questions, small groups inevitably arrive at the personal questions, the pièce de résistance, the time I always looked forward to because it gave me an opportunity to talk about myself.

During this time, people are usually encouraged to talk about how they sinned during the past week and then discuss how they can correct those sins in the future. Some will treat the occasion as a free therapy session by unloading their perceived personal struggles onto a group all-too eager to hear the gossip; others will obviously have nothing worthwhile to say and make up some ambiguous response about the "bad things" they did and how they want to work on "reading the Bible more and having a closer relationship with God."

For the latter kind of individual, I have observed a weird aversion to specificity at small groups. For example, men will often talk of their "impurity" over the past week, a term usually meant as a euphemism for porn and/or masturbation, though the vagueness of the word "impurity" could theoretically refer to any act from vulgar speech to rape. If people were truly interested in the improvement of their peers, they would encourage specificity in confessions. Instead, everyone wants the social benefit of seeming open and vulnerable without actually being open and vulnerable. It is far easier for a Christian to speak vaguely about ten sins they committed in the past hour than to admit to one specific and unglamorous misstep over the past month.

Even if someone does not think they sinned at all over the past week, they will nonetheless feel pressure to blurt out some ambiguous sin such as "impurity" when put on the spot, because the prevailing Christian narrative demands that everyone have sins to share.

In its most charitable interpretation, Christianity calls for self-improvement through the act of being born again, time and time again, into a better person. "All have sinned and fall short of the glory of God,"[42] so we should attempt to face our faults and not ignore them. The Church construes this potentially useful narrative of individual introspection into the bizarre idea that people sin all the time — every week, every day, in every hour — because humans are inherently sinful. The Church often says something along the lines of the following:

> "We are all born with a nature that *produces* sin. It is a fountain of sin. Like a deep-sea oil well spurting endless gallons of black oil into the ocean, the human mind, heart, and will keep producing sinful cravings, desires, and thoughts."[43]

> "It is doubtful that one can go 24 hours without sinning since we are all sinners (Rom 5:19) ... When we accept Jesus Christ as our Savior

and Lord, all of our past, current, and future sins are forgiven. But we still sin. How often do we sin? We sin so much that we do not know when we sin."[44]

The Church conflates sin as an act with sin as a state of being. Instead of thinking, "I have sinned, therefore I must be a sinner," the Christian thinks, "I am a sinner, therefore I must have sinned." Even if a small group member cannot point to any specific act against God they recently committed, the Christian narrative tells them that they simply are not looking hard enough. If, at every small group session, I found nothing wrong with the way I lived my life over the past week, then people would think there was something wrong with me. In reality, I would never dare admit that I had lived life righteously. Instead, I would come up with some banal and ambiguous story of sin because, paradoxically, sinning makes me seem like a better Christian so long as the sin is relatable and I feel bad about it. The Christian who admits to made-up sins will come across as humble and self-improving, while one who honestly shares their lack of sin will seem arrogant and blind.[45]

I agree that we should remain self-aware of our ever-present room for growth, but that is entirely different from asserting a narrative of constant sin regardless of our attempts to overcome it. Such a narrative promotes self-deprecation more than it promotes self-reflection. It seeks to convince us that we are, by our very existence, unworthy wretches who deserve a torturous eternity in Hell. It teaches that we are fundamentally incapable of saving ourselves from punishment, and that we must rely on the grace of an external being for salvation.[46] This is the opposite of empowerment, and it does no good for those seeking repentance.

Weekly gatherings where friends sincerely and concretely discuss their recent behavior hold great potential for promoting personal improvement. Such discussions of specific personal faults are often difficult — they require bare vulnerability and a brave willingness to change behavior. Many Christian small groups do not embolden their members to engage in these kinds of discussions. Why should a Christian confess with embarrassing honesty when they can achieve the same social reward by hiding behind trite descriptions of extremely general sins?

As it stands, small groups do not need to encourage personal improvement so long as they encourage the personal accumulation of guilt. Jesus will inevitably free the Christian of their guilt eventually, and that experience of entering the depths of unworthiness before resurrecting to a sense of powerful freedom stands among the most cathartic emotional experiences within Christianity. These moments of internal salvation are powerful, but they are easy. Lasting behavioral change is not easy, or cathartic, or comfortable, but it is ultimately what the message of Christ challenges us to pursue. If Christian small groups chose to focus on the salvation of individuals in this life rather than in an afterlife, no one would have to feel the shame and guilt that arises out of constantly convincing oneself they do not deserve Heaven.

CONCLUSION

Whether you call it Bible study or small group, the Christian routine of applying biblical passages to our lives with neat weekly goals fails to encourage a healthy approach to either studying the Bible or interacting in small groups. We should not read the Bible solely to apply it to our lives, we should read it to gain wisdom from an ancient text. We should not share life experiences because we need to pretend that we have sinned, we should share them because we want to honestly connect with our friends.

To fit in the Christian society, hide behind vague language, feel guilty, and repeat every week.

Chapter Five

The Emphasis on Evangelism

When a newcomer to the Church first attends Sunday services or weekly small groups, they could readily expect to hear something about evangelism. It is the *Evangelical* Church, after all. Even so, the newcomer may not expect the concept of evangelism to pervade the Christian lessons week in and week out. When the Church asks a Christian to live closer to God or to love their neighbor, in some way or another these virtues will eventually take the form of evangelism. The Church will constantly remind Christians, either explicitly or implicitly, that they hold a moral imperative to root the purpose of their day-to-day actions in persuading others to join the Church. They are taught that every co-worker, every friend, and every stranger should be thought of as a lost soul in need of conversion.

Because of the primacy of evangelism, Church groups tend to place an overwhelming emphasis on *how* to share what they believe rather than *what* it is they believe. With time and effort that could be spent learning about the teachings of Jesus, Christians are instead made to feel guilty for not evangelizing enough.

I think Evangelical groups place such accentuated emphasis on sharing the gospel because it is easy. I do not mean that the actual act of sharing the gospel is easy, but that *placing emphasis* on sharing the gospel is easy. It is easy to try and then fail to share the gospel with your friends, then go to a community that thrives on others sharing how they too tried and failed to share the gospel with their friends. Of course, someone will occasionally succeed in bringing a new member into the group, where they too can share in the sharing of the trials of sharing the Word. Why, after all, should anyone put in all the hard work necessary to understand what they believe when they only need to know that they must share whatever it is they do believe? If ever asked a difficult question, one can always just provide the answer of "faith."

Christians talk about sharing "the Word of God" as though all believers have a shared understanding of what "the Word of God" is. There are some ideas, however, that I think Christians should spend time clarifying amongst themselves before they go out to share their religion with the world. For instance, who wrote and compiled the Bible? What does it mean that Jesus is the "Son of God?" Is sin passed between generations the same way hair color gets passed from parent to child?

For the evangelizer, such questions of doctrinal substance are but distractions from the goal of convincing others to join the Church and gain everlasting life, though for many non-Christians hearing the gospel message, the answers to these questions are rather important. When evangelizing, many Christians seem to forget that their religion is not just a feel-good social club, but also an all-encompassing worldview that makes many strange and disconcerting claims.

Instead of rooting the persuasive power of their evangelism in the believability of dogmatic claims — which Christians never critically analyze and are therefore woefully incapable of defending — Christians speak instead about the general positive effects of the Christian life. The Church encourages believers to talk to their secular friends about the social benefits of joining a small group, or the sense of moral fulfillment that accompanies church-organized volunteer work. By ignoring the complications of dogma and basing their evangelical appeals on personal *effectiveness* rather than doctrinal *truth*, Christians unintentionally betray the fact of the matter: dogma is an unimportant and indefensible appendage to an otherwise appealing way of life.[47]

CONCLUSION

Evangelism as a concept contains no inherent fault. People often carry beneficial stories and experiences that they want to share with others, and it seems perfectly reasonable for societies to encourage the sharing of these positive messages. The Church, however, places so much emphasis on evangelizing the message of Jesus that it neglects to encourage a deep understanding of what the message of Jesus actually was.

To fit in the Christian society, always feel guilty for not evangelizing enough.

Chapter Six

The Inerrant Word

Imagine you go out to eat with your friends at a restaurant you have never visited before. On the way there, you proclaim, "I have read reviews online, and I believe the french fries at this restaurant are tasty." After placing orders and receiving food, you excitedly taste the fries only to find them so salty that everyone who tries them throws up in disgust. Your friends point out that you were incorrect in your prior belief about the tastiness of the food. Never one to admit a mistake, you insist that your friends are actually the ones who are wrong, for surely barf-inducing fries *must* be tasty. Confused and worried for your sanity, your logically-minded friends pull out a black board to spell out their line of reasoning:

1. The french fries at this restaurant are excessively salty and make everyone throw up.

2. Excessively salty french fries that make everyone throw up are not tasty.

3. Therefore, the french fries at this restaurant are not tasty.

Shaking your head in disapproval, you snatch the chalk from their hands and write your own deductive claims:

1. The french fries at this restaurant are tasty.

2. The french fries at this restaurant are excessively salty and make everyone throw up.

3. Therefore, tasty french fries are excessively salty and make everyone throw up.

Incredulous, your friends leave for a better restaurant as you self-assuredly sit alone, nibbling at the disgustingly salty fries. Perhaps redefining "good" in order to maintain an illusion of inerrancy isn't such a helpful idea.[48]

* * *

If a Christian were to stumble upon a long-lost religious text that seemed to make assertions of truth, they would surely scour every line of this new piece of literature, discuss it critically with peers, and seek to understand the perspective of the author before deciding whether the book contained any truth at all, let alone divinely inspired truth. However, if this religious text happens to be the Bible, then the good Christian's attitude shifts completely. In the case of the Bible and the Bible alone, Christians are expected to accept a text as inerrant simply because their pastor tells them to.

Statistics show that American Christians hold an astonishing ability to assert the inerrancy of scripture without ever reading it. Only 32% of American Christians claim to have read all or almost all of the Bible, yet 83% of American Christians say the Bible is either the literal word of God or the inspired word of God.[49] How is it that one can call a work of literature inerrant and divinely inspired if they have never read it? If one asserts that a text contains the sole source of absolute truth prior to reading the text, then the concept of truth becomes meaningless, and the claim, "the text is infallibly true," holds no significance whatsoever.[50] For the claim of inerrancy to mean anything, it must be falsifiable. Every Christian should ask, what could the Bible say such that it becomes errant? If not blatant historical contradictions, then what? If not justification of slavery, then what? If not divinely ordained genocide, then what else could make a text errant?

ON BIBLICAL ATROCITIES

Any Christian wishing to reconcile God's goodness with the lurid details of the Old Testament needs to perform an exceptional amount of casuistry to shift their definition of "good" such that it allows for clearly evil acts. Anyone who has read the Old Testament readily understands the horrors on show, and I see no need to provide extensive evidence for the rather obvious observation that heroes of the Old Testament engage in divinely ordained behavior that is abhorrent by any modern standard of morality. For those unfamiliar with the Old Testament, here is one example of what to expect:

> "They did battle against Midian, as the Lord had commanded Moses, and killed every male. ... The Israelites took the women of Midian and their little ones captive, and they plundered all their cattle, their flocks, and all their goods. All their towns where they had settled, and all their encampments, they burned, but they took all the spoil and all the plunder, both people and animals. ...

> "Moses said to them, "Have you allowed all the women to live? These women here, on Balaam's advice, made the Israelites act treacherously against the Lord in the affair of Peor, so that the plague came among the congregation of the Lord. Now therefore, kill every male among the little ones, and kill every

woman who has known a man by sleeping
with him. But all the young girls who have not
known a man by sleeping with him, keep alive
for yourselves."

– Numbers 31:7, 9-11, 15-18; NRSVue

When interpreting passages such as these, Christians are left in a bind. If these verses present an accurate account of history, then they erase any possibility
of a consistent or moral God. If the verses instead offer
an acceptable guide to morals, then Christians must
concede that the Bible's self-contradictory account of
history contains falsehoods and exaggerations like
many contemporaneous pagan accounts.[51] Christians
could, of course, avoid this bind altogether by aban-
doning the claim of inerrancy. They could treat the Old
Testament as a morally and historically flawed text that
nonetheless contains valuable lessons and cultural
context. Christians must choose their sacrifice: do they
follow a divinely inerrant text that shatters common
standards of morality and reason, or do they learn from
a flawed text that offers little in the way of absolute
truth?

Christians may choose to defend biblical inerrancy
by constantly changing the goalposts and persistently
altering the definition of "inerrant" such that it always

aligns with their creative scriptural interpretations. We could keep playing this linguistic game of cat and mouse forever, or Christians could choose to sacrifice the label of inerrancy for the reality of a text written by ancient humans who held beliefs far different from our own.

CONCLUSION

If you treat the Bible as a guideline for how to live your life, then you will find it clearly archaic and contradictory. If you think inerrancy means this collection of books always presents an accurate account of history, then I regret to say the Bible is errant on its face. Christians may nonetheless choose to call the Bible infallible as a convenient semantic maneuver, but clever wordplay does not change the reality of the text before us.

Now, if we treat this collection of documents as a historical literature of various genres and of various intents penned in certain times and places for particular audiences far detached from our own, and as writings that form a common thematic groundwork and a language of expression for the infinite to which we all relate and call God, then I don't know what errancy or inerrancy have to do with anything. We continue to read this collection of ancient books not because they

are inerrant, but because they ignite thoughtful consideration that can lead to personal and societal better-
ment.

**To fit in the Christian society, talk about the infallible
Word of God, but do not read it.**

Chapter Seven

The Art of Preaching

One under-appreciated aspect of Jesus' message is its ability to maintain persuasive power in text. No one has heard the inevitably persuasive voice of Jesus Christ, yet his voiceless teachings have nonetheless convinced modern disciples to follow his message just as ardently as those who heard his voice millennia ago. A good teacher maintains their power in writing; a good preacher cannot necessarily say the same.

Preaching is an art, one that utilizes the inflection of voice, loudness of volume, and gesturing of hands to deliver an emotionally affecting message, rallying together the Church society every Sunday and giving Christians a reason to socialize at the same place every week. The art of preaching, while undeniably profound and uplifting when performed correctly, has the potential to create less knowledgeable Christians who place more value on style than substance.[52]

I am, admittedly, performing some linguistic gymnastics to form a distinction between preaching and teaching; when a pastor preaches, they very often also teach people things. Nonetheless, there certainly exists a distinction between those pastors whose effectiveness flows from their content and those whose effectiveness hinges on their performance. To become a successful preacher — persuading through style and sitting high in the hearts of the Church society — I have developed four easy tips to help you along.

DYLAN'S FOUR TIPS TO SUCCEED AT PREACHING

Tip #1: Understand that your effectiveness is proportional to your certainty

Next time you listen to a sermon, keep note of how often the pastor says the words, "I think." Whenever a pastor chooses to acknowledge the inherently subjective nature of their views and admit that what they are saying is only an interpretation of the Word of God, not the Word of God itself, then the pastor becomes a less persuasive preacher. They do become a better teacher, but that is not our goal here.

If you think that a historical Adam and Eve walked the earth, drop the "I think" and simply say it as though it is the most certain fact in the world. If you don't think that gay sex is acceptable, then say that God doesn't think gay sex is acceptable. Whenever you can speak on behalf of God you should do so — it creates a more powerful effect. There is no need for nuance. Nuance never inspired anyone. People did not come to church to hear what someone thinks; they came to hear the unambiguous voice of God, so give it to them.

Tip #2: Treat each sermon as though it is everyone's first

An effective preacher should primarily aim to bring others to the saving knowledge of Jesus Christ, not to mature those who already hold that saving faith. Why try to gain deeper knowledge when the knowledge Christians already possess is good enough for eternal life? This saving knowledge requires no complex analysis of rarely heard stories or serious wrestling with contrarian opinions. The fundamental tenants of Christianity are simple, so your sermons should be simple. Never delve too deeply into the text lest you lose your audience in the weeds of substantive biblical knowledge.

Tip #3: Present everything with emotional urgency

Crafting an informative and thought-provoking sermon every week is hard, so take that mediocre sermon you have written down and bring it to life with the presentation. Say some words softly and slowly, and then say others loudly and quickly. It doesn't matter which words, just throw in some random emphasis and inflection. People don't really care what you say so long as it makes them feel good.

For instance, you can read a story or parable of Jesus, then restate it verse-by verse with dramatic flare, taking random pauses between words. Once you have re-explained the short passage that already explained itself well enough the first time, make some relatable real-world connections to the present day. The modern day connection does not need to hold up to any scrutiny, just make sure you present it in a way that sounds coherent and impactful. If you have some extra time left to fill, a dramatic and impromptu altar call is always a hit.[53]

Tip #4: *Always bring it back to sin and repentance*

At the end of every lesson, from your interpretation of any biblical story, you should always challenge the audience to think about sin in their lives. Tell your congregation that they all sin constantly but don't offer any details as to how they sin, how you know they sin, or how they should atone for their sins apart from generally being a good person. Never, ever, be too specific about the sin or repenting — broad statements make more people feel personally impacted.

Make sure everyone feels guilty and then give them the catharsis of feeling free from the guilt you just created — free by the grace of God. It does not matter if your lesson was about Jesus or Jehoshaphat — everyone should feel guilty by the end of every sermon and repent. The story is always about us, and it is always about what we can do this upcoming week to avoid sin.

CONCLUSION

I do not mean to make light of the difficult job pastors face. I do not envy their position or the pressures they face from the Church community. That said, I cannot help but notice far too many bad teachers on the pulpit who resort to empty preaching and formulaic sermons that treat congregations like children. I find nothing at all wrong or invalid in impactful spiritual experiences garnered from effective public speaking, but eloquent preaching should not replace substantive teaching.

To fit in the Christian society, deliver sermons that are emotionally effective before they are true.

Chapter Eight

The Name of Jesus

Stay around a group of Christians for any extended period and you will notice that they use the name of Jesus *a lot*. Of course, this makes sense to some extent — Jesus Christ is the central figure in Christianity, and Christians claim to have a personal relationship with him. I nonetheless find it fascinating that Christians use the name so predominantly when they could just as easily use alternative, and often more appropriate, expressions of deity, such as 'God,' 'Lord,' or 'Father.' Nothing in this observation is inherently critical, only I suspect that it points to deeper problems with the overly simplistic way Christians tend to think about God.

JESUS AS FRIEND

In seeking a personal relationship with the Lord, Christians are naturally drawn to the most relatable part of their triune God: the human part. Even though he no longer walks this earth, Jesus maintains a kind of human approachability within Christan tradition. He is characterized as a personal savior and even a friend.[54] Unlike God the Father, Jesus the Son is unquestionably good. That is not to say God the Father is not good, only that he is not *unquestionably* good. Scripture characterizes the Father as good in a divine, incomprehensible sense, but certainly not "good" inasmuch as we generally understand the word. Jesus the Son sits just across from you preaching atop a hill; God the Father sits mysteriously across infinity. Jesus the Son heals the sick, reconciles the lost, and is himself the truth and life; God the Father allows the righteous to suffer, teaches lessons with death, and is a force to be wrestled with. Jesus the Son is a teacher and mentor to his disciples, his friends. God the Father is the all-powerful God of Job, the wrathful God of Joshua and Judges; He is indiscernible and unapproachable. The Son gives, the Father gives *and* takes away.

By overwhelmingly thinking of God as a human friend, one misses out on the full nuance of the God concept described in the Bible. I think the strange overuse of Jesus' name may point to many Christians' failure to truly confront the more distant, mysterious, and confusing characterizations of God expressed in the Old Testament.

JESUS AS SELF

A very prominent concept in Christian theology is the duality of Jesus Christ — that he existed simultaneously as fully human and fully divine. Christians treat Jesus' duality as some distant concept reserved for theologians, but when participating in the Church today, I readily see the dual nature of Jesus everywhere. Within the Church, the person of Jesus exists as two distinct psychological characterizations: the visceral, symbolic, divine characterization, and the grounded, historical, human characterization. The Jesus who believers call out to during the spiritual high of their favorite worship song is not the same Jesus who they examine when reading the book of Luke at Bible study.

The personal, powerful, and non-historical understanding of Jesus held within all Christians gets expressed most apparently in artistic portrayals of Jesus. No person knows what Jesus of Nazareth looked like, and artists have always had to rely on the Jesus who exists within them — a Jesus who is inevitably shaped by their own experience and culture. You will notice that when white people go about painting Jesus, they tend make him white as well. When Chinese Christians decide to paint Jesus, they often paint him with an Asian complexion, and so on for all other global Christian traditions.

Russian icon by Simon Ushakov (1677)

East Syriac Church painting of Jesus (9th century)

A mural (1951) depicting the baptism of Jesus in a typical Haitian rural scenery

Reconstruction of the enthroned Jesus (c. 10th-century East Central Asia)

Understanding Jesus the human is difficult and in-accessible to most — it requires time-consuming study of numerous historical accounts as well as background knowledge of the specific Jewish culture Jesus lived within. A historical conception of Jesus is not the one that has inspired billions to join Christianity. Jesus the *idea*, on the other hand, is exceedingly simple to understand. The symbol of Jesus anthropomorphizes universal concepts of love, sacrifice, and forgiveness, which followers are free to apply to their own lives and societies wherever they see fit. One does not, for instance, need to know the historical details of Roman crucifixion to understand the power in the image of God on a cross.

The personal accessibility of the Jesus idea is, in many ways, a wonderful thing. It allows diverse cultures to take a powerful narrative and easily adapt it to their circumstances. It provides many with a language of expression for sharing and processing profound spiritual experiences. That said, fully embracing the subjective Jesus comes with its costs. An over-emphasis on the psychological Jesus, unbound from biblical texts, allows individuals to artificially legitimize their own ideas by pretending that they are the ideas of God. As an example, take the ever-so-low-hanging fruit of the aggressively homophobic Westboro Baptist Church. Members of this 'Christian' institution regularly protest against homosexuality at public parks, universities, and — most disgustingly — LGBTQ funerals.[55] They perform such hateful actions because they claim to follow Jesus. As I hope we all know, the acts of the Westboro Baptist Church bear no relation to the teachings of Jesus the human, but this Church does not follow Jesus the human — they follow their idea of Jesus. Instead of shaping oneself to the mold of Jesus, many have shaped Jesus to the mold of their own prejudiced selves.

The spiritual and the historical conceptions of Jesus will inevitably feed off each other to some extent, though we should not be so quick to fully conflate the two identities. If we do not ground the concept of Jesus in some kind of historical reality, then Jesus becomes infinitely interpretable by those wishing to use the name of God as a tool for their own agendas. We cannot hope to follow the way of Jesus when the person of Jesus has become a mere extension of the self.

CONCLUSION

Ideally, Christians follow the teachings of the historical Jesus, which tell us to love liberally, give freely, and sacrifice readily. The conceptualization of God in the person of Jesus certainly serves a helpful and loving purpose, but this conception of God is not the only useful one that exists. If Christians continue to use the name of Jesus in a way that erases any distinction between the concepts "God" and "Jesus," then they cease to speak or think in a way that allows them to understand the challenging depths of the Hebrew God found in the Bible. The way we talk about God inevitably shapes the way we think about God, and the beautiful simplicity contained within the name of my friend, Jesus Christ, fails to adequately encapsulate all the uncertain complexities of this world.

Consistently using the name of Jesus to refer to God is not inherently wrong or harmful; it is simply counterproductive to a deeper understanding of that which we call God.

To fit in the Christian society, say "Jesus" whenever you might as well say "God."

Chapter Nine

The Power of Prayer

It is May 2020, and I have spent the first three months of lockdown isolated in my parents' house. After many hours of deep introspection that I never before had the time to engage in, I had just arrived at three unsettling realizations: 1) I did not legitimately think that an afterlife existed, 2) I had not legitimately thought that an afterlife existed for the better part of five years, and 3) I had been too afraid to admit this lack of conviction to anyone, even myself. For a life defined by the Church and a soul determined to live according to the way of Jesus, these unwelcome realizations constituted a deathblow to my status as a "true Christian." I did not want to abandon the God who had shaped my life so profoundly, but I knew I could no longer lie to myself about what I did and did not think. In clear distress, with nowhere to turn, I fell to my knees in my childhood room and prayed to God.

Prayer is believing that a conscious creator of the universe alters reality out of concern for the inner life of a particular human being; the whole idea of it lacks reason or sense. I think we should do it anyways.

A personal prostration of humility and surrender before a higher power is a deeply human act. The Church rightfully encourages this. Unfortunately, it also encourages another type of prayer — a social display of buzz words and egotism performed before a silent crowd. Christian society's posture towards both personal and social prayer deserves careful unpacking.

PERSONAL PRAYER

Within the Church, I see two common views of personal prayer put forth. There exists the religious view of prayer, wherein a supernatural God physically alters the world in the ways we desire, and then there is the secular view, in which the significance of prayer rests solely in its personal effect of peace and surrender. Kierkegaard describes the latter view succinctly. He writes, "The function of prayer is not to influence God, but rather to change the nature of the one who prays."[56] These two views on prayer are mutually incompatible, yet you will often see the same person accept both views in different states of mind.

Within the intellectual sphere of a Bible study or seminary class, espousing the secular view of prayer will make one appear wise, thoughtful, and respected. When in such a state of serious intellectual discussion, it becomes simply impossible to rationally defend the religious view of prayer, which rather quickly dissolves into a discomforting 'mystery' the moment one subjects it to critical thought. A rational, secular understanding of prayer recognizes that reality as we perceive it hinges on the stories we tell ourselves and the deep-rooted biases we often neglect. Under this line of thinking, prayer can legitimately change reality, not because an omnipotent God changes it for us, but because the act itself can shift the mental thought patterns that shape our existence. This secular understanding of prayer is coherent, nuanced, and utterly reasonable, and yet it lacks all the comfort and cosmic significance that makes the religious understanding of prayer so pervasive within the Church.

When the worship music plays and churchgoers lift their hands in the air, or when friends and family lay their hands upon those who have endured great tragedy, here the religious conception of prayer comes into full view. In such moments of religious ecstasy or heavy emotion, Christians will instinctively trust that their prayers fall upon the ears of a Heavenly Father willing and able to bend reality to the desires of His children. The purely internal view of prayer that many accepted at last week's Bible study gets thrown aside for emotional certainty in a loving God.

There are, of course, inherent advantages to those positing a supernatural power in prayer. If the distraught child cries out, "Lord, please free my grandmother from her cancer," which argument feels more immediately appealing? The argument that says their prayer served only to shape their subjective outlook on the world, or the argument that says God will now actually help heal their grandmother? If someone decides to remind the child that their words serve only to enact change in themselves and not in a higher power, they could not expect to find many friends within their Christian circle.

Christians' shifting view on prayer reveals, rather plainly, Christian society's prioritization of emotional comfort over intellectual consistency. So far in these essays I have promoted the idea that the Church should alter its approach to religious beliefs to make room for rational considerations of truth; in the case of personal prayer, I am not so sure this is the argument I wish to make. In a healthy society, sometimes we need to prioritize emotion over intellect. Duplicitous attitudes towards prayer may well exist as a valid exercise of belief, of acting as though something is true despite not being fully convinced. Perhaps prayer changes me and not God, but only when I earnestly hope that it also changes God. Whatever the fact may be, the psychological complexities of prayer warrant an attitude of humility before a great mystery, not certainty in a supernatural wish-granter.

SOCIAL PRAYER

If you have ever attended a Sunday service or weekly small group, you have almost definitely observed social prayers — those times when individuals pray aloud to an audience, usually at the beginning or end of a biblical lesson. Nothing is intrinsically wrong or misguided in these public expressions of prayer, which have been part of the Christian tradition for millennia, but what I find problematic is the performative way in which Evangelical Christians tend to go about making these prayers. When delivering a public prayer, one in the Evangelical Church is encouraged to speak eloquently and with the 'correct' Christian phrases. The kinds of prayers that I was rewarded for — the kinds that led to compliments and pats on the back from Christian leaders — were those in which I made a concerted effort to use language that made me sound righteous and intelligent. I was not compelled to ever verbalize honest vulnerability before the Lord.

Consider this prayer, which comes from the introduction of a random sermon — the first publicly available recording I could find online:

"Father, we thank you for the opportunity to administer to these, your precious sheep. Thank you, Lord, that revelation knowledge will flow freely, uninterrupted and unhindered by the satanical demonic force. Father, I pray that you will speak through my vocal chords and think through my mind. None of me, all of you. And we give you the honor and the glory and the praise. Anoint every ear to hear. Anoint me, Lord, to teach it, to share it. Under the anointing of God, we welcome you.

In Jesus' name, Amen."[57]

Prayers such as these are often not meant to serve as a personal outpouring of one's innermost self, but rather as a method to prime an audience for a religious message. Such a rhetorical method may have its place, but it is worth remembering that prayers spoken aloud to a large audience take on an entirely different form and purpose from prayers uttered only to oneself. With social prayer, one is forced to face the inevitable insecurities of public speaking. "What will others think of me? How loudly should I speak? Will I stumble over my words?" The social pressures of public prayer often lead Christians to stray away from offering an unguarded personal outpouring (which is risky and potentially awkward), and instead rely on the crutch of tried-and-true clichés. The goal of social prayer is usually not to strengthen a connection with God, but rather to present a "good Christian" image.

Christians will often strain to saturate their public prayers with religious buzzwords, because this type of contrived language tends to impress other Christians. In the above quotation, you will see phrases that appear in no language other than Christian-ese: "anoint every ear," "precious sheep," "unhindered by the satanical demonic force." This is not how normal people speak. When someone chooses to put aside the linguistic grandstanding and pray aloud with honest vulnerability, without pretenses or concerns for maintaining a manicured Christian persona, the Church often does not know how to react. It is a powerful and unsettling experience in the Christian society, and one that is exceedingly rare. Christians should consider if they really want to continue diluting a concept as potentially profound as prayer by encouraging social posturing and meaningless buzzwords.[58]

CONCLUSION

I believe prayer has power. It has immense power to change our outlook and our actions, to remind us of our ultimate place of surrender before powers we cannot control. Christians would agree that prayer holds great power, though that statement means very different things to different Christians, or even to the same Christian in different states of mind. Whatever one thinks of personal prayer, all those in the Christian society will tacitly agree that prayer holds the great power of social advancement, of seeming like a good Christian with good Christian words. Prayer can be a brave expression of individual vulnerability, but Christians have chosen to use it as a formulaic tool for social conformity.

To fit in the Christian society, pray carefully, pray confidently, and pray so that others may hear you.

Afterword

THE WALK OF THE BORN AGAIN

We begin our faith walk with the excitement of the Spirit and the conviction of our favorite Hillsong track. We are eager to join the community of Christians and eager to share the new knowledge we possess. We feel as the Samaritan Woman did in evangelizing Christ's message with only the little he had given her.[59] Perhaps we pretend to know a bit more than we really do. With a childlike faith, we believe that God is on our side, and that He is wholly and unquestionably good. We accept the existence of the infinite and believe that it concerns itself with even the smallest trials of our day to day. We believe in the infallibility of the Bible but have yet to read it for ourselves. Our understanding of the Lord is immature, yet we possess great confidence in the supernatural influence He wields over our lives. We are more than motivated to passionately evangelize what we believe.

Then, perhaps, we start asking questions, the kinds of questions that make those in our Bible study uncomfortable, that they label as doubts, and whose conventional answer is usually some vague appeal to faith. We begin to read the Bible closely and question the claims of inerrancy made by our energetic and entertaining pastor. What do we do with these difficult questions that challenge the very foundations of our faith? Perhaps we ignore them, and fight to stay rooted in our shallow but certain soil. Perhaps we abandon the religion entirely. Or, perhaps, we keep asking questions.

Over time we begin to know that we know nothing, and the chaos of life reveals itself as incommensurable with our simplistic Christian narrative. The Lord used to be our best friend who answered our prayers, now He sits across infinity. We used to find the supernatural within the mundane; now life seems so prosaic. We find ourselves in the position of Job, trembling before a God who is far greater than we can comprehend. We become like Abraham, fearful before a God whose commands seem appallingly paradoxical. We are afraid, as the infallible truths instilled in us by our Christian society begin to give way to unwelcome realizations. God is no longer a wise man sitting in the clouds, but we do not yet know what He is exactly. We only know that there is far more work to be done.

All too often, moving onward along our walk of faith means leaving behind our Christian society. For all the Church has given us in meaningful relationships, it has taken from us in the suppression of individual thoughts and opinions. The Church remains enjoyable, friendly, and genuinely loving, but it now feels like a step backwards from our pursuit of truth and maturity. Maturing in faith very often means sacrificing our Christian reputation for a deeper understanding of truth. It means moving away from the Church and closer to God.

SOCIETY AND TRUTH

In many of our most famous stories you will find a struggle between social conformity and truth. From Orwell's *1984* to Pixar's *The Bug's Life* (not to mention the biblical accounts of a guy called Jesus), our stories characterize the hero as someone who sacrifices social acceptance in favor of a higher truth. Social pressures in the real world very often do act in opposition to the pursuit of truth, but it depends entirely on the kinds of societies we create. Christian societies can remain enjoyable, friendly, and loving while also becoming non-dogmatic and open to critical questioning. We do not need to sacrifice the truth found in reason for spiritual experiences found in community.

Church congregations could easily encourage truth-seeking by providing clear avenues for individuals to critically discuss weekly sermons. Currently, any discussion of biblical interpretation relies on brief and uncritical post-sermon chit-chat. As I make my way to the parking lot after a Sunday service, I might walk and talk with a friend, opining about how applicable and thought-provoking the sermon was. This substance-less discussion will last for about five seconds before we quickly shift to talking about organizing lunch plans at the local Panda Express. A handful of congregations I have encountered ask that attendees stay after the sermon, eat lunch with their peers, and critically engage with the message they just heard. These organized discussions only manage to yield productive conversations when Church leaders establish an explicit expectation that attendees should bring their own ideas, questions, and disagreements.

Here is another relatively simple step in the right direction: Christians could tell more stories. Christians could open the Bible and critically read more of the stories within it, even those confusing ones in the Old Testament. They could even study non-biblical stories that nonetheless contain thought-provoking ideas. For whatever reason, Christians are only taught detailed biblical narratives as children in Sunday School before they graduate to the formulaic three-point sermons preached at them as adults. Stories aren't just for kids, so we should read them, critically and without the need to apply them to our everyday lives or root their value in their historicity. Christians could believe in more stories, with a meaningful belief that leads to substantive changes in behavior.

* * *

If there is any unifying link between the various critiques and observations I have covered, it is a conviction in the power of individuals to shape their societies. Moral hierarchies are *choices*. The meanings of words are *decisions*. Definitions of belief, faith, and doubt are not set in stone; the current forms of prayer, preaching, and evangelism are not inevitable. Every person gets to choose the behaviors they reward, punish, or ignore in others, and while many do not make these decisions consciously or intentionally, no one should ever pretend that these choices do not continually exist, that we go about life powerless to define our societies. Christians get to decide what it means to be a Christian, and Evangelicals have continually decided that belonging to Christianity means pursuing dogmatic conformity. I do not think these Christians understand the damage their decisions have wreaked on the reputation of Christ and his followers. They have taken a diamond and turned it into coal.

And yet, I cannot deny the fact that so many of my most valuable memories come from my time within the

Church. I cannot ignore that so many of the people I most love and respect call themselves Christian. I understand and appreciate the good that Christianity has given me, but I am tired. I am tired of navigating the Christian society, of saying the right things. I am tired of sermons that read like bad high school essays, where the so-called analysis of Scripture is just summary infused with emotion. I am tired of people pretending that they know more than they do, and seemingly reducing everything to sin, repentance, and evangelism. I am tired of Christians telling me that a life of faith is a life of fearless certainty.

I do not want to abandon Christianity. I still want to perform acts of service with my friends; I still want to find spiritual fulfillment in song and prayer. I do not want to throw the baby out with the bath water, but I just must ask: why is there so much bath water? I observe a definite good in the Christian society, one that had kept me coming back time after time; I also observe much that makes me glad I chose to leave.

Now that you know how to fit in the Christian society, I pray you never do.

Notes

1. See Ephesians 6:5-8, Colossians 3:22-25, Titus 2:9-10, 1 Peter 2:18, and 1 Timothy 6:1. If the authors of the New Testament were not true Christians, no one was. Consider also that the whole of U.S. slave owning society in the 19th century was Christian and used the Bible to defend the practice.

2. Quakers would fit this latter category of undogmatic Christians.

3. See the words of Jesus in Matthew 18:20: "'For where two or three are gathered in my name, I am there among them.'" (NRSVue) Some form of community is a necessary component of the religion.

4. John 14:6

5. John 8:44; Ephesians 6:14

6. For data on the crisis of friendship in the U.S., see Daniel A. Cox, "The State of American Friendship."

7. And also not be gay. That's important too.

8. See John 3:16: "For God so loved the world that he gave his only Son, so that everyone who believes in him may not perish but may have eternal life." (NRSVue)

See also Romans 10:9. "If you confess with your mouth that Jesus is Lord and believe in your heart that God raised him from the dead, you will be saved." (NRSVue)

9. How they know this, I am not entirely sure, other than they wish it to be true.

10. Schacter and Scarry, "Mining the Past to Construct the Future: Memory and Belief as Forms of Knowledge."

    "We consider it extremely unlikely that beliefs are expressed in the brain as sentence-like data structures."

11. Worse yet, a new believer may conceive of something like the ill-translated Japanese conception of Christ, "Dainichi," which means 'sun of god' instead of 'Son of God.' Early Jesuit missionaries in Japan initially thought that these Japanese believed in Jesus, but the form of the Jesus idea was completely different from the idea the missionaries held.

    See Aldo Tollini, "Translation During the Christian Century in Japan."

12. I do not believe dense philosophy is required to be convinced of the apparent reality that words hold different meanings to different people. That said, many great philosophers have explored semantics rigorously, and I think some of their ideas are worth noting. For

instance, among Wittgenstein's key insights in *Philosophical Investigations* was the observation that we do not need to know the definition of a word to use it in speech or writing. The meaning of word is not determined top-down by an objective definition, but rather bottom-up through individual observations in the way a word is used. Thus, words themselves hold no platonic meaning, but rather words' meanings to individuals emerge through their usage throughout the life of the individual. Quine follows a similar line of thinking to Wittgenstein, emphasizing the mechanisms of social reinforcement that shape the meanings of words (see *Word and Object* §2). Other theories of semantics lead to similar conclusions on the significance of the individual mind in creating meaning. Within a theory of reference, Bertrand Russel distinguishes "logically proper names" from "abbreviated definite descriptions." As an example of an abbreviated term, take a name such as "George Washington." When I say "George Washington," I usually mean to refer to the first President of the United States. George Washington *could* refer to someone or something else, but to know this, precise descriptions of the intended referent must be included in the communication. A statement such as "I will live forever in Heaven" includes various abbreviated definite descriptions with their logically proper names obscured by the brevity of the claim. If individuals were to spell out in excruciating detail the logically proper names of "live," "forever," and "Heaven," then I suspect people would discover that they mean slightly different things when they say the sentence,

"I will live forever in Heaven." Alternatively, people might discover that they themselves do not know precisely what the words they are stating refer to.

13. In this section, I am careful to specify that I am considering whether people can choose their convictions, not whether people can choose their beliefs. It is a slight distinction that will not matter to some, but I use this language because I think that the word "conviction" holds a more definite meaning than the word "belief." Intuitively, most people understand that beliefs can reside on a spectrum ranging from complete conviction to complete doubt. One could argue that, with enough internal willpower, individuals might be able nudge the needle of belief along this spectrum and become *more certain* in a given idea, even if they do not become *completely certain*.

I think there are at least two problems with this possibility. For one, this potential ability for people to nudge their beliefs along a continuum does not affect my argument with regard to Christianity, because Christianity is ultimately concerned with pushing adherents towards a state of absolute conviction. Upon our deaths, Christian doctrine implies that God will map our spectra of belief onto binary outputs corresponding with Heaven and Hell. That is to say, the moment someone internalizes a specific amount of certainty in the idea that Jesus rose from the dead, a supernatural switch will flip to allow them into a heavenly afterlife when they die. Where exactly along the spectrum of belief God decides to flip the switch, no one can say. Christians can only know that anything less than full conviction in God-given truths puts their eternal fates into doubt. For a deeper exploration of the Christian social pressures that reward expressions of certainty, see chapter 2: The Concept of Faith.

Secondly, the question of whether someone can nudge their thoughts into a greater sense of certainty requires one to accept the terms of a flawed abstraction. The metaphor of belief being akin to a needle moving along a spectrum is just that: a metaphor. It is reductive and inherently limiting. This framing of belief follows a spatial model, wherein someone's current state can be conceptualized as a point in n-dimensional space with a certain distance from another point. To say that someone is 50% certain of some proposition's truth implies that the individual's belief point is some distance away from the point of certainty. This idea of beliefs existing at a definite point in space requires 1) that there exist certain objective variables defining belief, and 2) that the values of these variables could be precisely determined. By saying that someone has successfully "nudged the needle" of a belief towards a more certain state, we are saying that they have altered the value of some variable pertinent to belief such that the distance of their belief point is now closer to the point associated with complete conviction.

To put this concretely, we can think of someone who has denied the existence of a god for many years suddenly falling to their knees in prayer. Since praying to a god is likely a variable contributing to belief in a god, and since this person's prayer variable has shifted in a direction of increased belief, we can say that the praying person's belief in a god is now closer to the point of full conviction.

The problems with this spatial model are, 1) the concept of belief is socially constructed, meaning that there are no objective variables defining belief, and 2) even if there were objective variables, those variables would be qualitative and impossible to reliably reduce to a single point in any quantitative space. The patterns of neuron firings that define our existence do not map nicely onto some objective idea-continuum. Our thoughts just are what they are. Our brains simply function as they function. Any attempt to apply objective value judgments to our internal mental world is doomed from the start.

You might notice that the problem of metaphorical abstraction applies to complete convictions just as it applies to in-between beliefs — neither exists as any objective thing with an objective definition. To get around this problem, we can think about conviction purely subjectively. When I write that someone is "convinced" in some proposition, I mean that they are convinced based on a standard of conviction they themselves have defined. In this way, if a person thinks that they are absolutely convinced in the truth of a proposition, then I take this to

mean that they really are absolutely convinced in it —
there is no objective measure, only a subjective one.
With this in view, my argument in this section about
choosing conviction can be more precisely articulated
as the following: If someone internally expresses doubt
in the truth of a proposition, then they cannot will
themselves back into a *sense* of certainty without some
new source of external information.

If this endnote seemed to add confusing complications
to an otherwise simple model of belief, that is sort of
the point. Human thought is complicated and murky
— treating it any differently is a mistake.

14. Luther's Works 54, 424

15. The thought experiment of Igor the elf is exactly akin to
the famous thought experiment of Russell's Teapot.
Bertrand Russell imagines a person who claims that
there exists a teapot orbiting the sun in an elliptical or-
bit between the Earth and Mars. He uses this thought
experiment to make an argument about how the bur-
den of proof rests on the person trying to prove a
dogmatic claim and not on the person trying to disprove a dogmatic claim, but he could just as easily
have made an argument about the meaninglessness of
such a teapot even if it did exist.

16. We should keep in mind that there is no objective
standard for the qualities one must exhibit in order to

be a "true believer." The actions associated with a belief will shift depending on the society one resides in. For example, if I were to tell people within a Protestant Christian society that I believe in the Virgin Mary, then they would accept by statement as true belief without looking for any further behavioral proof. The Protestant Church does not emphasize this dogma very much. Now, if I were to profess belief in the Virgin Mary within a Catholic society, then those within the church would not accept my stated belief as fully legitimate unless I performed certain other actions. I would need to pray to Mary, revere statues of Mary, and maybe even put an image of Mary in my house. Both Protestants and Catholics may hold the same individual conviction that Mary gave birth as a virgin, but that conviction is more behaviorally meaningful to Catholics than to Protestants. A meaningless belief in one society may be meaningful in another.

17. For an example of a Christian academic asserting Daniel as the author of the book of Daniel, see Finley, "Who Wrote the Book of Daniel?"

18. Sims, "Daniel," 327, "The consensus of modern biblical scholarship is that the book was composed in the second century B.C., that it is a pseudonymous work, and that it is indeed an example of prophecy after the fact."

Tucker, "Daniel: History of Interpretation," 131, "Critical study resulted in a near consensus view of a Maccabean date for the book in its entirety…"

See also, Davies, Daniel.

19. When I asked my pastor about why he believes in Daniel's historicity despite its irrelevance to the sermon he just delivered, his answer was simply, "faith." See Chapter 2 for an exploration of why such an answer is unsatisfying.

20. The mere declaration of a belief does hold *some* significance towards the fostering of a tribal sense of belonging. By the shared utterance and repetition of historical dogma, Christians create stronger communities within their churches, but this sense of belonging is not at all created by the actual content of the professed beliefs. Christians could take any claim at all and make it just as meaningful as the historicity of Daniel simply by repeating it enough and asserting it as religious dogma. It is not, therefore, the claim of historicity that makes historical beliefs socially meaningful, but rather the fact that they are widespread and heavily accepted.

21. For those interested, scholars theorize that ancient flood stories from the middle east were influenced by an actual flood in the Mesopotamian basin.

Mallowan, "Noah's Flood Reconsidered."

22. Hume, "Sceptical Doubts Concerning the Operations of the Understanding."

23. The event I am describing is the writing on the wall during King Belshazzar's feast, as described in the book of Daniel, Chapter 5.

24. Seow, *Daniel*; Tucker, "Daniel: History of Interpretation."

25. This is to say nothing of the fact that human experience is not always a reliable source of truth. Ask the nearest hippie tripping on shrooms.

26. The Evangelical Church *could* establish more significant behavioral expectations for dogmatic belief, but it chooses not to. This is especially true for belief in an afterlife.

    American Evangelicals could do what Mormons or Jehovah's Witnesses have done and decide that true belief in an afterlife necessitates missionary work, but they have not done this. Evangelicals certainly celebrate those missionaries who have made brave efforts to evangelize, though such efforts are not required to demonstrate true belief. Evangelical Christians only require that one consistently profess belief in an afterlife. No further action is required beyond that.

    These minimal requirements for belief in an afterlife are rather strange considering the significant implications of the Christian afterlife. I invite you to honestly consider how someone's behavior might change if they became truly convinced in the idea that they would live forever in Heaven whilst their atheist next-door neighbor burned in Hell. As far as I am concerned, if someone with any moral compass whatsoever became convinced in the Christian afterlife, then they would devote their entire lives on earth to ensuring that as many people as possible avoid an eternity in pain. Some Christians do behave in this way, but many do not.

For so many dogmatic beliefs within the Church, there are no reasonable ways someone could conceivably express their beliefs in action other than to simply make a statement of conviction, but when it comes to belief in an afterlife (one of the only Christian dogmas that should reasonably transform someone's entire existence) Christians still decide that mere statements suffice for true belief.

For an empirical look at the insignificance of dogmatic belief on behavior, see Chapter Three's discussion of research by political scientists Putnam and Campbell.

27. In some languages there is no distinction at all between the concepts of faith and belief — they *literally* mean the same thing. In German, for instance, "Glaube" means "belief," but it is also the closest translation for "faith."

28. The rapture refers to the idea that true Christians will fly into Heaven during some future end times. The idea comes from 1 Thessalonians 4:16-17: "For the Lord himself, with a cry of command, with the archangel's call and with the sound of God's trumpet, will descend from heaven, and the dead in Christ will rise first. Then we who are alive, who are left, will be caught up in the clouds together with them to meet the Lord in the air; and so we will be with the Lord forever." - (NRSVue)

29. The next section, "Faith as Certainty," goes into more detail on how Christians define faith. Spoiler: they define faith as certainty.

30. To clarify, I think that the statement, "I believe because I have faith" may be a legitimate and meaningful assertion. If we take the conclusions of the last chapter to heart, then belief means "meaningful action." Further, as I discuss later, faith could mean "a force of will that allows one to follow a narrative despite doubts." Therefore, the statement, "I believe because I have faith" could mean, "I perform certain meaningful actions because I possess a force of will that allows me to follow a narrative despite my doubts." This statement seems quite reasonable to me.

That said, when Christians actually say a statement such as, "I believe because I have faith," they often refer to dogma with no meaningful action attached to it.

The Church by-and-large asserts a definition of belief relating to conviction rather than action, meaning that the sentence, "I believe because I have faith" means the same as "I am convinced because I am convinced."

31. Joyce Meyer, "Fighting Fear with Faith."

32. gotquestions.org, "Faith vs. Fear - What Does the Bible Say?"

33. Hour of Power with Bobby Schuller, "Faith Is the Opposite of Fear."

34. I should note that the book of Esther is unique in that God is not mentioned once. Therefore, strictly speaking, God did not call on Esther to do anything, though common Jewish and Christian interpretations consider Esther to have been an agent of God who acted in faith.

35. See Luke 22:44. See also Matthew 26:36-46 and Mark 14:32-42 for the other accounts of Jesus in distress at Gethsemane.

36. Kierkegaard, *Fear and Trembling*.

Under Kierkegaard's analysis, the story of Abraham binding Isaac communicates that individuals exercise true faith only when they stand in individual opposition to universal norms of society. When Abraham proceeds with his plan to sacrifice Isaac, he shirks any reasonable moral code on the conviction that God told him to perform the act. Kierkegaard noted that if such an act to follow God is considered moral, then morality ceases to serve a purpose. Faith is, in this way, paradoxical and necessarily individual. "So even if someone were so cowardly and base as to want to be a knight of faith on someone else's responsibility, he would never become one; for only the single individual becomes one, as the single individual, and this is the knight's greatness (99)."

37. For those curious, the refrigerator did not contain the oat milk I believed it would contain. This was very sad.

38. In a much-referenced story from Genesis 32, Jacob physically wrestles with God. Christian leaders will use this story to argue that Christians should wrestle with their doubts just as Jacob wrestled with God. This usually comes with the assumption that God will inevitably come out on top. Read the story from Genesis, however, and you will find that God *loses* the wrestling match with Jacob.

39. It could reasonably be argued that no fact claim *ever* compels action on its own, and that action in response to a fact requires some value judgment. If I believe that my next-door neighbor's house is on fire, we might think that this belief alone is sufficient to compel my action of dialing 911, but it is not; I need to also possess

belief in the moral imperative that helping one's neighbor is a good or obligatory act. Without this value belief, I will take no action in response to my fact belief that my neighbor's house is on fire.

This line of argument also works the other way: value beliefs need fact beliefs in order to manifest in action. If I never believe that my neighbor is in need (a fact belief), then I will never see a chance to act on my value belief that helping one's neighbor is a good or obligatory act. It seems reasonable, therefore, to argue that value claims are not more meaningful than fact claims, because the decision to act always requires the conjunction of a value belief with a fact belief.

So why is this argument flawed? In my view, it takes some unnatural linguistic maneuvering to say that the observation of an event amounts to a belief. It is true, in a sense, that if I observe a house on fire then I believe the house to be on fire, but this is not how people normally think or speak. Belief usually implies that 1) someone thinks a claim is true, and 2) that claim is not immediately obvious. If someone sees a burning house and states, "I believe that house is on fire," we would probably think them a little slow. Instead, someone would probably just state, "The house is on fire," because there is no need to believe in something that their senses clearly communicate to them. If we think of the act of observation as something different than the act of believing, then we find that value beliefs may be meaningful on their own, without any accompanying fact beliefs.

For example:

Observation: My neighbor's house is on fire.

Value belief: One ought to help others in need.

Action: I call 911.

To a large extent, the philosophical complications I have introduced in this footnote are a moot point — they do not practically apply to Christianity. Many dogmatic beliefs in Christianity do not compel action under *any* reasonable value belief. For instance, under no reasonable value system does belief in Moses' authorship of the Pentateuch result in a change of behavior beyond statement.

Fact Belief: Moses wrote the Pentateuch.

Value Belief: ?

Action: I verbally state, "Moses wrote the Pentateuch."

In sum:

1) Every value belief can meaningfully influence behavior when it is accompanied by a relevant observation or fact belief.

2) Not every fact belief holds the capacity to meaningfully influence behavior, because not all fact claims have an accompanying value claim through which they compel meaningful behavior.

40. Putnam and Campbell, "Religion and Good Neighborliness."

41. This paragraph in particular — and the whole book in general — owes itself to the work of Jonathan Haidt in *The Righteous Mind.* It is essential reading for anyone with beliefs.

42. Romans 3:23

43. Open The Bible with Pastor Colin Smith, "We Sin Because We Are Sinners."

44. NeverThirsty.org, "Is It Possible for Someone to Not Sin for 24 Hours?"

45. In the biblical story of Job, after Job has lost nearly everything in life, he correctly maintains a conviction in his own righteousness. Job's friends, however, contend that something must be wrong with him. In their view, sin must exit, because sin is what causes suffering. Like Job's friends, Christians will often contend that faults exist in others regardless of how righteously those people behave.

46. The colloquial telling of Romans 5 in "The Message" version of the Bible puts the common self-deprecating Christian view quite well:

"[Jesus] presented himself for this sacrificial death when we were far too weak and rebellious to do anything to get ourselves ready. And even if we hadn't been so weak, we wouldn't have known what to do anyway. We can understand someone dying for a person worth dying for, and we can understand how someone good and noble could inspire us to selfless sacrifice. But God put his love on the line for us by offering his Son in sacrificial death while we were of no use whatever to him." (Romans 5:6-8, The Message)

For more examples of self-deprecating language in Christianity, see the lyrics to popular Christian songs. For example:

- "Amazing Grace" ("how sweet the sound that saved a wretch like me")

- "How Deep the Father's Love" ("To make a wretch His treasure")

- "Reckless Love" by Cory Asbury ("I don't deserve [the love of God]")

47. Nietzsche called this persuasive fallacy of conflating doctrinal effectiveness with doctrinal truth "the demonstration of power." It describes when "a thought's truth is demonstrated by its *effects* ... that which a man finds delightful, that for which a man sheds blood must be *true*." (Italics in original)

Nietzsche, *God Is Dead. God Remains Dead. And We Have Killed Him*, 25.

48. The two arguments in this analogy would take the following form when explicitly applied to biblical inerrancy:

    1. The Bible is a text that presents historical contradictions and condones morally reprehensible behavior.

    2. A text that presents historical contradictions and condones morally reprehensible behavior is not infallible.

    3. Therefore, the Bible is not infallible.

    1. The Bible is an infallible text.

    2. The Bible is a text that presents historical contradictions and condones morally reprehensible behavior.

    3. Therefore, an infallible text may present historical contradictions and condone morally reprehensible behavior.

49. Smietana, "Lifeway Research;" Gallup Inc., "Fewer in U.S. Now See Bible as Literal Word of God."

50. To drive this point home, consider that there are two uses of the word "is" in the English language: an "is" of predication and an "is" of identity. The sentence, "The sun is hot," uses the word "is" to ascribe a property, "hot," to an object, "the sun." This is the "is" of predication. Now take the sentence, "The sun is the

star at the center of our solar system." In this case, "is" serves to indicate that the subject of the sentence is identical to the predicate, such that in every case I use the phrase "the sun," I could just as well say, "the star at the center of our solar system." This is the "is" of identity.

In any sane interpretation, the sentence, "The Bible is inerrant," uses an "is" of predication, but many Christians treat that claim as containing an "is" of identity. To them, if the Bible says x, then x must be true, even if x does not seem true by any normal understanding of truth. Biblical inerrancy does not assert that truth is a property the Bible holds, rather they claim that the Bible defines truth.

51. Enns, *The Bible Tells Me So*; Earl, *The Joshua Delusion?*

52. As David Hume wrote, "Eloquence, at its highest pitch, leaves little room for reason or reflection, but, addressing itself entirely to the fancy or the affections, captivates the willing hearers and subdues their understanding."

53. For those unfamiliar, the term "altar call" refers to a direct appeal by a pastor for non-Christians to convert to Christianity.

54. See the hymn, "O What a Friend we Have in Jesus."

55. To see more details on the hatred of the Westboro Baptist Church, you either visit their official website, godhatesfags.com, or you can simply notice that their official website is godhatesfags.com.

56. Søren Kierkegaard, *Upbuilding Discourses in Various Spirits*, trans. Howard V. Hong and Edna H. Hong, vol. 15, Kierkegaard's Writings, XV (Princeton University Press, 2009).

57. Dollar, *The Purpose of Suffering - Sunday Service*, 00:01.

58. Churches do not have to perform social prayer in a top-down, pastor-led form. I appreciate the prayer tradition in some Latin American Church communities, which I had the opportunity to experience for myself while on a mission's trip in rural Guatemala. In this tradition, members of a community form a circle and pray aloud all at once in a cacophony of overlapping voices. There is no social posturing or Christian-ese — no one cares what anyone says, no one even understands what the person next to them is saying. Such a tradition of prayer encourages a personal connection with the divine amidst friends, all without the need for social posturing. I think the American Church could learn something from it.

59. See John 4.

References

Aldo Tollini. "Translation During the Christian Century in Japan." *Between Texts, Beyond Words*, December 2018. https://doi.org/10.30687/978-88-6969-311-3/001.

Daniel A. Cox. "The State of American Friendship: Change, Challenges, and Loss." *The Survey Center on American Life* (blog), June 8, 2021. https://www.americansurveycenter.org/research/the-state-of-american-friendship-change-challenges-and-loss/.

Davies, Philip R. *Daniel*. Edited by R.N. Whybray. London, United Kingdom: Bloomsbury Publishing Plc, 1987.

Dollar, Creflo. "The Purpose of Suffering - Sunday Service," Creflo Dollar Ministries, recorded September 23, 2022. Video of sermon, 1:25:23. https://www.youtube.com/watch?v=lmOYo2Y9X5s

Earl, Douglas S. The Joshua Delusion?: Rethinking Genocide in the Bible. Cascade Books, 2011.

Enns, Peter. *The Bible Tells Me So: Why Defending Scripture Has Made Us Unable to Read It*. Reprint edition. HarperOne, 2015.

Finley, Tom. "Who Wrote the Book of Daniel? (Part 1)." Biola University Blogs, February 4, 2022. https://www.biola.edu/blogs/good-book-blog/2022/who-wrote-the-book-of-daniel-part-1.

Gallup Inc. "Fewer in U.S. Now See Bible as Literal Word of God." Gallup.com, July 6, 2022. https://news.gallup.com/poll/394262/fewer-bible-literal-word-god.aspx.

References

gotquestions.org. "Faith vs. Fear - What Does the Bible Say?" GotQuestions.org. Accessed March 26, 2024. https://www.gotquestions.org/faith-vs-fear.html.

Haidt, Jonathan. *The Righteous Mind: Why Good People Are Divided by Politics and Religion*. Reprint edition. New York: Vintage, 2013.

Hour of Power with Bobby Schuller. "Faith Is the Opposite of Fear." Hour of Power with Bobby Schuller, April 14, 2019. https://hourofpower.org/faith-is-the-opposite-of-fear/.

Hume, David. "Sceptical Doubts Concerning the Operations of the Understanding." In *An Enquiry Concerning Human Understanding*, 1748.

Joyce Meyer. "Fighting Fear with Faith." joycemeyer.org. Accessed March 26, 2024. https://joycemeyer.org/Grow-Your-Faith/Articles/Fighting-Fear-with-Faith.

Kierkegaard, Soren. *Fear and Trembling*. Translated by Alastair Hannay. Reprint edition. London: Penguin Classics, 1986.

Kierkegaard, Søren. *Upbuilding Discourses in Various Spirits*. Translated by Howard V. Hong and Edna H. Hong. Vol. 15. Kierkegaard's Writings, XV. Princeton University Press, 2009.

Mallowan, M. E. L. "Noah's Flood Reconsidered." *Iraq* 26, no. 2 (1964): 62–82. https://doi.org/10.2307/4199766.

References

NeverThirsty.org. "Is It Possible for Someone to Not Sin for 24 Hours?" NeverThirsty. Accessed March 26, 2024. https://www.neverthirsty.org/bible-qa/qa-archives/question/is-it-possible-for-a-man-or-woman-to-go-24-hours-without-committing-a-sin/.

Nietzsche, Friedrich. *God Is Dead. God Remains Dead. And We Have Killed Him.* Translated by R. Kevin Hill and Michael A. Scarpitti. Penguin Books, 2021.

Open The Bible with Pastor Colin Smith. "We Sin Because We Are Sinners." Open the Bible, October 16, 2021. https://openthebible.org/open-the-bible-daily/we-sin-because-we-are-sinners/.

Putnam, Robert D., and David E. Campbell. "Religion and Good Neighborliness." In *American Grace: How Religion Divides and Unites Us.* New York, NY: Simon & Schuster, 2012.

Quine, Willard Van Orman. *Word and Object.* The MIT Press, 2013. https://doi.org/10.7551/mitpress/9636.001.0001.

Schacter, Daniel L., and Elaine Scarry. "Mining the Past to Construct the Future: Memory and Belief as Forms of Knowledge." In *Memory, Brain, and Belief*, 11–32. Harvard University Press, 2001.

Seow, Choon-Leong. *Daniel.* 1st edition. Louisville, KY: Westminster John Knox Press, 2003.

Sims, James H. "Daniel." In *A Complete Literary Guide to the Bible*, edited by Leland Ryken and Tremper Longman III, Second Impression edition. Zondervan Academic, 1993.

References

Smietana, Bob. "Americans Are Fond of the Bible, Don't Actually Read It," April 25, 2017. https://research.lifeway.com/2017/04/25/lifeway-research-americans-are-fond-of-the-bible-dont-actually-read-it/.

Tucker, Wade Dennis Jr., PhD. "Daniel: History of Interpretation." In *Dictionary of the Old Testament Prophets*, edited by Mark J. Boda and J. Gordon McConville. InterVarsity Press, 2012.

Wittgenstein, Ludwig. *Philosophical Investigations*. Translated by G.E.M. Anscombe. Basil Blackwell, 1953.

Image Attribution

Pg. 89

Thank you very much for reading. I hope this book inspired thought and sparked conversation.

If you enjoyed what you read, please consider leaving a review on your preferred platform.

-- Dylan